Katihar TO Kennedy

THE
ROAD
LESS
TRAVELLED

Katihar to Kennedy

THE
ROAD
LESS
TRAVELLED

SANJAY KUMAR

Katihar to Kennedy

Vani Book Company
Head Office

4695, 21-A, Daryaganj, New Delhi 110 002, India
Phone +91 11 23273167 **Fax** : +91 11 23275710

Registered Bookstores and Offices

Ashok Rajpath, Patna 800 004, Bihar
Coffee House Campus, Mahatma Gandhi Marg, Allahabad 211 001, Uttar Pradesh
Mahatma Gandhi International Hindi University, Wardha 442 001, Maharashtra
Moti Park Opp. Water Tank, Sultania Road Bhopal 462 001, Madhya Pradesh
Goripur Taliya Para, 313, R.B.C. Road 24- Parganas (North) Kolkata 743 166, West Bengal

www.vaniprakashan.in
marketing@vaniprakashan.in
sales@vaniprakashan.in

Katihar to Kennedy : The Road Less Travelled
by Sanjay Kumar

ISBN : 978-93-89012-63-7 (Hardbound)
Autobiography

First Edition 2019
Price : ₹ 499 / **$ 12.99 / £** 8.99

Printed and bound in Yash Printographics, Noida
Vani-Prakashan's signature motif is created by Artist Maqbool Fida Husain

For Maa and Babuji who couldn't finish their schooling but worked relentlessly to help me weave my dreams. You both sent me off on my educational journey from Katihar with your belief in me and your trust. I am infinitely happy not to have let you both down and to have travelled up to Harvard instead. My journey is an extension of your courage and grit.

Contents

Contents

Contents

Foreword

It's a pleasure to read through Sanjay Kumar's journey from a government high school in a small town of Katihar, in one of India's economically backward districts, to the Harvard Kennedy School in Cambridge, Massachusetts. While the journey in the days of modern communication and transport is no longer onerous, the psychological journey is an immense one. The chronicles of such intrepid souls as Sanjay add much to the societal discourse of how we might promote such universal values as fairness and equal access to opportunities for those cut off from the economic and social mainstream in their milieus.

I met Sanjay only recently when he began working as the India Country Director for the Mittal Institute at Harvard – an entity dedicated to connecting Harvard University with all the countries of South Asia, prompting two-way intellectual exchange – that I have had the privilege of directing for some time now.

The book helped me understand in some detail the crucible experiences that have shaped Sanjay. One can see his many endearing character traits emerging from these experiences including a freedom of spirit that allow him to sample life's experiences freely, unconstrained by the limitations of Katihar, and to not recoil from failure, but to treat it as something from which to learn. There are many endearing private joys that he reveals. These are a privilege to witness through the transparent lens of Sanjay's memories. As Sanjay notes in his chronicles, we are each where we are as a result of the efforts of many who propelled us along, and hopefully we will extend to others similar favors. Sanjay certainly lives up to that ideal. It's an important part of why we value him as a team member at the Mittal Institute.

While writing this short foreword, I tried to think about why the book resonates with me. First, my academic work over the past two decades is consistent with the broad arc of Sanjay's experiences. Given a chance, there is amazing talent lurking in society's interstices, usually far from the glare of the mainstream. It behooves those of us more fortunate than others to find ways to uncover the talent of which Sanjay is an exemplar. Second, through work with talented young entrepreneurs with whom I co-founded the global talent assessment company, Aspiring Minds, we see that in countries where we operate – India, China, US, Philippines and others – overlooked talent outside of metropolitan areas abounds and is, sadly, left mostly undiscovered. Had good fortune not smiled on Sanjay, of course with much effort on the part of several, he might easily have had his potential overlooked. This is what makes Sanjay's story so relevant to numerous others, not just in India, but across the world.

Let me close with a more recent personal anecdote. With colleagues at Harvard, I recently helped start a pro bono one week academic and professional 'experience' for young folks who are first-in-family to college from across the developing world. My colleagues and I, supported by Harvard alums primarily from the Gulf Cooperation Council countries, have run this program twice (2017 and 2018), with much logistical help from the Mittal Institute. Last year, we received so many applications that the selection rate for attending was under 2% after a very rigorous selection process. The selected youth came from 25 odd countries in Eastern Europe, Central and South Asia, MENA region (Middle east and North Africa) and elsewhere in Africa. It was one of the most amazing teaching experiences I've ever had, simply because the kids were, for the first times in their professional lives, given a chance to dream, unconstrained by their circumstances, and were predictably enthusiastic and high-energy. These young men and women will accomplish all that people like Sanjay can, and we all hope, even more!

Hopefully Sanjay's narrative will inspire others from origins like his to embark on their own, no doubt unique, voyages of discovery. Hopefully the narrative will also inspire those of us, like Sanjay and like those reading this preface, to do what we can to make those journeys easier for others.

Tarun Khanna
Cambridge, MA
January 16, 2019

Acknowledgements

This book is definitely a gift of my educational journey. I would like to acknowledge my deep gratitude to all my previous schools, colleges, and universities. It was all these institutions that helped me grow as a learner throughout life. All these Institutions provided me with an identity, as their student I will always remain indebted to them. Teachers at different stages of education did not only contribute to my learning during class, but later too, in retrospect. They have been invaluable mentors.

I am extremely thankful to the teachers of Harishankar Nayak High School, High School at Semapur, and St. Xavier's school. Teachers at Hindu College and Satyawati College will always remain special for me as they played a most important role in empowering me as solid Political Science student. The JNU faculty were crucial in facilitating the expansion of my thought. Whatever foundation I could built as a student was mainly due to their teaching and my interaction with them. Some of the things a few of them said truly remained in my heart forever. I was rarely a favorite student but almost all were generous and supportive.

Prof. I. N. Mukherjee, my M.Phil and Ph.D. supervisor was my longest-serving teacher, and with whom I have had the opportunity to deep-dive into research and earn my precious degrees.

At Harvard University's Ron Heifetz, Tim MacCarthy, Tim O' Brien, Jeni Klugman, Rahul Mehrotra, Kasturi Rangan, Robert Lawrence, Quinton Mayne and Michael Ignatieff were amazing. Martha Chen, Martyben, with whom I had the privilege of both working at the grassroots level in India as well as being part of her class at Harvard Graduate School of Design, is amazing. From all of them, besides book and theoretical learning, I learnt the highest levels of professionalism in the classroom. I will always remain indebted to each of them. I would like to thank Suzanne Shende, Program Director of Mason Program for her support during the Harvard period.

I would like to thank Faculty at the ISS, The Hague, who opened the gates of my curiosity.

This long journey has been taken through my family's support and has been their dream too. It is their unconditional love and support that motivated me to aim bigger and higher. They are all part of the journey and hence of the book. My eldest brothers Arunbhaiya and Arbindbhaiya, always acted as my immediate guardians. It was their love and fear that helped me grow gently and stay out of messes in Katihar and in Delhi. My sisters, Anita didi, Reeta didi and Sangita have been the as stalwart as sisters can possibly be, throughout the years. My brothers-in-law and sisters-in-law have been always very supportive. My cousin Rameshbhaiya always stood by me whenever I needed emotional support. I am indebted to all my uncles and aunts; cousin brothers and sisters from both paternal and maternal sides for their love and affection especially through the early years of my childhood and adolescence. All of them taught me love and compassion.

Major K.P. Singh deserves special mention for his love, affection, and unconditional support for me. Rajesh bhaiya and his father, Sh. R.U. Singh, a retired IAS officer, guided me and helped me professionally while I was navigating Bihar. Kulwinder Kaur, faculty at Jamia Millia Islamia and Sagar Preet Hooda, IPS, have been constant sources of inspiration and a great support in my endeavors. Sanjaya and Ajay Mark from Woodstock School, Mussoorie touched my life with their special affection and provided me with necessary logistical support for finishing a major part of the book in Mussoorie. They remain family-philosophers-guides to me.

I am thankful to Andy and Libby who always encouraged me to finish this book and supported me in all my endeavors. My nieces and nephews extend me unconditional love and make my life joyful. Sharing this book with them extends me lot of hope from my next generation. I am thankful to thousands of government school and college students I keenly observed. They are the ones who inspired me to pen down my journey so they could believe in the improbable. I will always remain indebted to them, who shared their school and college stories with me.

Seema deserves special mention not only because she is my wife but she has been my closest critic and challenger. She has been the strongest support in my adult life, and I am in awe of her energy. Seema's father, mother, and siblings provided me lot of support during our years of struggle. I shall always remain indebted to them. Chaitanya and Tathya are my closest allies in fun, games, and all the unusual conversation around life at home. I am extremely thankful to the almighty for gifting me these two, sweetest kids!

No life journey is exciting without the presence of friends. Good or bad, they add value to our lives. I learned many life skills with friends from JNU and Delhi University that I never learned in the classroom. I am not listing everyone's name here but I will stay indebted to my classmates and batchmates at Hindu college and Satyawati College, hostel-mates and the roommates for their support outside my family. JNU gave me so many younger brothers. They were my extended family members and will always remain in my memory. Some remain special for their unconditional support.

Friends from Katihar will always have special place in my heart. Some of them are mentioned in this book but many of them are not. Through this acknowledgement I would like to thank all my classmates, seniors, and juniors from Harishankar Nayak and St.Xavier's School for all their love and affection.

I feel fortunate to have Acharya Jagadish and Chachi in my life. He is not only an Acharya for me but he became a father figure for me.

Women members and grassroots leaders of SEWA had a special impact on my life. I learned the most of all through their struggle and successes. Women leaders of Jehangirpuri, Raghubirnagar, Sundernagri, and other parts of Delhi, Bihar,

Rajasthan, Uttarakhand, West Bengal, M.P., and Gujarat inspired me with their extraordinary courage and positivity. I will always be indebted to the SEWA movement for making me a solution-driven and action oriented individual. It infused activism in my blood for which I would always be grateful. Elaben, the founder of SEWA, is the most simple and strongest woman I have ever come to known in my life. I had the privilege of learning many things from her. I was also fortunate to have Renanaben as my mentor during my SEWA years and she was the one who harnessed my potential and provided me with the opportunities which were precious for my growth as an activist, a professional, and a grassroots worker. Manorma-ben always remained a great support and a motherly figure during my time at SEWA. Colleagues from SEWA days will always remain special for me.

The batchmates and friends from Harvard added a new flavor and energy into my life. They will always remain very special in my life. The Harvard Alumni Network is one of the biggest assets I have acquired through life. I will always remain grateful to the Ash Centre for providing me with the scholarship to support my studies at the Kennedy School. I will always remain indebted to Tim Burke and other colleagues at the Centre for taking good care of me during my time at Harvard.

Colleagues from The Lakshmi Mittal and Family South Asia Institute including Tarun and Meena entrusted me with a very big responsibility, to establish and expand the work of institute in India. I shall always remain grateful to both of them. Farhana has been one of my most dependable supports over the past few years. I would like to thank all my colleagues at Harvard University for their constant support while I deliver on my current responsibilities.

Last but not the least, I would like to thank Vani Prakashan for their extraordinary faith in me and my story. Their decision to publish this book as part of their maiden venture into English speaks a lot about their generosity and trust. Aditi's belief in me and my journey opened the door of our collaboration. She has been blessed with an immense capacity to connect with people and patience to explore possibilities.

I am sure this book is just a beginning of a stronger relationship. I shall always remain grateful to Saumya for editing the book and agreeing to be part of the project as a whole. I would also like to thank Shoaib bhai for giving me a beautiful cover page. This book is would not have been possible without the team work of Vani Prakashan Group, their editorial and marketing teams and the administration.

Chapter One

The Beginning

You and I, we travel through time. Through my own journey I have seen time bring about drastic changes - situations and results I could have never foreseen. I have seen utter darkness transform into vibrant, iridescent dawn and I have seen dust settle to reveal visions of grandeur which seem otherworldly. Fickle and unpredictable, time is constant in its commitment to turn, twist, and test.

My tests in life began early, and failure paved my way to success. I had, like most Indians, extremely humble beginnings. I lived in a small town with an almost invisible existence – Katihar – a dusty, chaotic place in the interiors of Bihar, which had yet to wake up to anything forward and modern. We lived in huts, the kinds extremely poor story book heroes inhabit before their fortune turns in a rags to-riches rigmarole. My story is not precisely rags to riches, but does today seem a fantasy in its own right.

I had been written off. Long before my potential, aptitude, acumen, and interests could be evaluated, I had been written off by well-wishers due to academic failure. My story is not just that of a rise above one failure, but that of overcoming fear of failure. This book is a journey through several important junctures in life, each with its own share of fascination, learning, disillusionment, and its own transition to the next. The grand jigsaw of life only makes sense retrospectively, and here I am, pulling all the pieces of the puzzle apart, to see how they make sense.

It was spring, 2015. I was sitting in the Kennedy School library, looking out of the window, a little before graduation. The gentle rustle of golden leaves in the school lawns was like hypnotic music, which drove me deeper into the world of my own reverie. A moment later, the plush landscape of the Kennedy School had transformed into the dusty, rustic, narrow alleyways of Katihar. Wasn't it just yesterday I was running around directionlessly on the streets of my hometown? How surreal then that I sit here today, in this prestigious institution, surrounded not by my relatives' unsolicited demotivation but by rows and rows of books inscribing much of the knowledge mankind has accumulated over centuries? Katihar to Kennedy – how did this become possible? It seems like the plot for a Bollywood drama. And looking back, my life definitely reads like it.

* * *

Katihar is a small, somnolent town in Bihar, officially counted among the 115 backward districts of India. It isn't difficult to explore the entire town on foot; I know Katihar's lanes, roads, houses, shrubs, trees and every possible physical landmark like the back of my hand. As is the case with most small towns, everyone knew everyone. With a population of around 1,50,000 during our childhood, most faces were familiar, neighbors thrived on the affairs of other homes and everyone had a say in everyone else's life.

It is not what you would call a progressive or modern settlement; quite the opposite. In early adolescence, the parochial psyche and customs of my native land only seemed natural. Back in my town dreams are marred by limits and concerns of practical existence. As understanding of the world dawned, some latent part of me struggled to break through these suffocating boundaries and chase an as yet formulated dream.

We were a family of eight sharing our sparse hut. My uncle's family stayed with us in that scant space, but somehow we all fit together.

Our home was situated close to a railway colony, many inhabitants of which were Bengali. I played with a lot of Bengali boys growing up, and ended up fluent in Bangla. Learning and understanding different cultures was, one might say, an adolescent habit. This need to learn about and appreciate diverse only grew with time, and my pursuit of them has proved endlessly rewarding, whether they be experiences of local migrants or the melting pot feel of global, multicultural terrains.

The hut was not to remain my home for long. My father soon purchased some land close to the railway colony. There, with much diligence and care, he built a few semi-pucca rooms. It wasn't a fancy home, but it was a leap up from where we had begun. In time we transitioned from this to a cement-and-bricks construction – a proper pucca house.

Through these transitions, while our family faced many tribulations subsisting on my father's meager income, life was beautiful and exciting. I have grown up in localities with a very strong sense of community. Often, right after the twilight hour, inhabitants sauntered out of their homes and formed little groups alive with animated conversation. They huddled together, discussing various topics and sharing lived experiences. Winters were even more wonderful, when these huddles began to center round bonfires. Elders broke into song accompanied by the enthusiastic thumping of basic percussion instruments. We were alive and together. My young mind absorbed all this fondly. Even to date the tunes break into my head and take me back to that time spent in the company of community, family, and my father.

My father was my hero. He was 5 feet 8 inches in height, and handsome by any standards. He led a simple life, with a fondness for good food, good clothes, and good music. Simple, but good. He was a meticulous man, always looking after his belongings with great care. We didn't have any almirahs or fancy wardrobes, so all his clothes were neatly folded and placed carefully inside a briefcase – day after day. He literally lived out of a suitcase.

Among these sparse belongings was a harmonium and a radio. His attachment to music was powerful. Indian music soothed him and film songs were favorite listening. We owned a gramophone, and later bought a tape recorder too. The luxuries of my childhood existence are shaped by music. Our entire family waited eagerly for Wednesdays, when Binaca Geetmala, hosted by the iconic Ameen Sayani, aired. It seems inconceivable today, but all of us huddled close around the single radio since the volume was low and none of us wanted to miss the musical countdown. What a contrast from the personal device driven families of today.

My father was hardworking. He was always on the move. He worked as a Munshi with a leading Marwari business family in town. Owing to his continued hard work and far-sightedness, he was eventually able to open a dhaba in partnership with my uncle. The dhaba ran smoothly for a while, but then my father diversified into working as a food supplier for the railway hospital. Perched on his bicycle, he rode dutifully around, fulfilling his responsibilities. I never saw him idling. He was always planning ahead, keeping the family in the centre of his vision.

Babuji was our idol, but Maa, she was the one who we spent more time with. She held the family together through sheer care. In Babuji's absence she kept a close eye on what each one of us was doing. Clad in plain sarees, she was a housewife, and took great pride in ensuring her family was well-fed and well-nurtured. Neither Maa nor Babuji could complete their schooling, but both ensured their children got the best education they could afford. Maa took care to prepare us well for school and hand over a lovingly prepared tiffin. Even when we ventured outside Katihar to pursue further education her love poured out in snacks and sweets she happily prepared and packed for us. Her act of packing food had of course another objective – she didn't want us to go hungry on days pocket money fell short. Homecooked food came to our rescue on many occasions.

My mother was good with economic decision making. She managed even to support Babuji, who often borrowed from Maa's savings. While living a simple life themselves, they ensured the best for us. Education was always an important subject with them, and Maa and Babuji wanted us to do well. Very well.

* * *

What makes the premise of this Katihar to Kennedy story different, I think, is that despite such a firm focus on education within our modest family, it was the academic turf I floundered outstandingly on. Shame, a broken spirit, and a halt of dreaming – I went through it all. However, while I was expecting life to plummet still lower, it swung around and I was resuscitated. Not just resuscitated; I am writing from the hallowed premises of the most sought-after educational destination in the world. And just this is not it either. Along the way my experiences defied expectation and this proclivity for unexplored horizons remains irrepressible. In the process, and despite its clichéd sound, I discover myself anew, repeatedly. Katihar to Kennedy is a journey both within and without.

It is a quiet day in the library. The exams are over and most students are roaming around the gorgeous campus, breathtaking when I stop to stare. Peeping out from behind the glass window and looking around at the world I feel a strong sense of privilege. I also know this privilege has been backed by years and years of relentless hard work.

It is a balmy day. The sky has a light hue of blue, covering the entire world, it seems, in a blanket of optimism. The yard is closed for construction as the school readies itself for physical expansion. A few days ago, while attending a ceremony for beginning the construction process, I heard eminent academics emphasize the importance of state-of-the-art infrastructure to enable the best learning ecosystems on campus. What I could gather from their speeches was that they did not look at this construction activity as mere physical expansion. They held a bigger vision for the future, which reflected a fierce concern for constantly providing their students with the best – in terms of curricula, mentorship, books, research opportunities, as well as hard infrastructure. In their vision, the physical was being constructed to aid the psychological – *a structure to help enable minds and harness their talent and potential.*

What a contrast from my beginnings! From a clear dearth of basic needs to this place rich in thought, perspective, and access to resources, it has been an extraordinary journey. Though they have also had infinitely more money to work with, it is perhaps (and largely, therefore) true that leaders in education have had a very different approach to building institutions in this part of the world. They have been innovative, meticulous, and caring. Institutions in India present a less heartening picture. Lack of care and initiative, along with the absence of vision and direction, is destroying precocious minds and youthful potential.

Education is a lifelong process. Formal learning happens through institutions, but we learn a great deal more through our experiences and through the social machinery around us. Both the good, and the bad. My case is similar. I began by learning in structured institutions, many of which suffer from a dearth of resources, some of which offered visions of more that only fuelled greater hunger for expanding my mind. I have, however, learned a lot from social interactions, traveling, observing people, animals, and nature. I have had the opportunity and the privilege to interact with an learn from the socially marginalized, the middle-class, as well as the rich and the privileged.

In fact, until I left my hometown, I did not know the meaning and the importance of 'resources'. Narrow, dusty roads, broken and unfinished buildings, squalor and dirt and constrained mindsets – all of this was natural and real. I was introduced to other kinds of realities, first in Delhi, then at Harvard. International exposure helped consolidate my understanding of people, their mindsets and scope for growth based on different levels of education, access to resources, and the psycho-social environment around them. There is much to learn through multi-cultural interactions, for which I am indebted especially to Harvard.

* * *

I have, throughout, been inspired by people's stories. Ostensibly great people. Obscure people. People I read about. People I met. People I worked with. People I worked for. Everyone around me gave me an opportunity to understand life and its nuances. People's stories are rich in struggle, perseverance, courage, emotion high and low, and each is an inimitable lesson to learn from. When all these elements are woven together they create a powerful narrative–something capable of igniting, empowering, influencing, or motivating someone else. We learn best when we learn from stories, and I decided to pen my own biography as I read those of others. The specific physical, emotional, and educational landscapes I traversed have, I hope, resonance or impact for the young and the old. From a precarious moment of failure and humiliation through perseverance and passion, life has come a long way, bringing much illumination. Education is engagement for me, and I firmly believe the process is not complete till one has passed on all one has learned to others. Here is my attempt.

The Acharya who taught me meditation proposed that the purpose of life should be "atma mokshatam" and "jagat hitaycha". Besides attaining salvation for ourselves it is our duty to work for the welfare for others. This book is my personal meditation, and a loan of hope.

My Sanskrit teacher in school used to tell our class, "Vidyarthi ke jeevan mein kabhi Monday nahin aata aur pehli taareekh nahi aati hai." He meant students cannot waste time waiting for a prescribed date to begin learning. Now is the time for action. I failed to understand then; I get it now.

Katihar to Kennedy – the phrase might suggest grandiose intent, but this book is really just about the lessons I learned – from failures as well as from moments of triumph. Lessons I learned while engaged most intimately with harsh socio-economic realities, and contrasts I experienced, moving between cities, institutions, and job roles. It is also a book of honest confrontation, of my own ego and pride. During the closing ceremony of the Kennedy School's Mason Program, Jamil Mahuad, an ex-President of Ecuador delivering the keynote, remarked that "It is the steps that are important, not just the feet." I think I understood this better too when I was forced into introspection by my failures. I value my successes in perspective, in relation to my failures. And since the complex machinery of life keeps moving, I have also always focused on the next challenge at hand rather than wallowing in transitory self-congratulation or mortification.

Here is my journey, as bare and honest as possible. I hope it resonates with some of you. I hope it gives you something to remember, something to love, and something to hold onto when your own path seems uncertain and bleak. ❑❑

Chapter Two

Small Town Boy

One afternoon I got back from school brimming with excitement. It was the summer of 1983. I threw my bag on the bed and began pacing from one corner of the house to the other, desperately waiting for Babuji. Today was going to be a special day. When Babuji got back he was going to take me to the market to buy the most wonderful gift of my short life – a bicycle! This was going to be my first individual possession. A bicycle, no ordinary toy. In the life of a 10 year old, this was a mammoth event. I remember each detail of the day vividly.

Maa, and all three of my sisters especially, participated in my excitement as though it were their own. They always did - my joys were theirs, vicariously. Finally I could stand being indoors no longer, and raced outside, to catch him soonest he was home - I raced up to him as I saw him approach. Yes, yes, he was totally up for it! He pulled me onto the bar between his seat and the handlebars and took me to Mangal Bazaar on his own bicycle. We meandered through wayside shops before reaching Daulat Raam Chowk. Aggarwal Cycles was one of the biggest dealers and retailers of Hero cycles in town. But Hero bicycles were too expensive. We found a shop which also sold Avon cycles, which Babuji's budget could just about afford. I remember checking out bicycle after bicycle, testing them. I remember the blue bicycle I selected for myself. It was an Avon bicycle - the brand was sturdy and no-frills, quite popular back then.

Babuji's parenting, though frugal and disciplined, was careful to anticipate the needs of a growing child. This cycle became my fondest companion. I started riding it to school, and the blue bicycle won me quite some cool among friends. I was among the few people in our batch who owned a bicycle, and now I had something to flaunt.

Babuji's gift will remain forever special. He was himself a man of few possessions. A few clothes, a harmonium, and a cycle to commute to and in town. He did dream of owning a car someday, but had to settle with a motorbike, and that too as his sons' or others' pillion rider. But now I, his son, all of 10, had a blue bicycle of my own, which I proudly rode around on, flaunting it as 'mine'.

* * *

I was reminded forcefully of this incident with my son Chaitanya in Cambridge. Having noticed his flair for the computer sciences and his expertise with applications, I was keen to support his advancement in the best possible way. He had already begun coding in Scratch, which was supposedly not easy for a 5th grader to pick up. An idea sprang to mind. Seema, my wife was surprised when I suggested it, but agreed. A MacBook was a big financial investment, but we decided to get him one. We wanted to encourage our son's skills, enable him to the web, and aid him in his sound recordings; Chaitanya had begun pursuing music passionately.

When we brought the MacBook Pro home and gifted it to him, he was shocked. He couldn't believe it was for him. He was elated, yes, but wasn't convinced he deserved it. Seema and I just asked him to make the most of it, and explore on his own terms. Soon Chaitanya was tutoring juniors at school in Scratch.

My father infused joy into the process of going to and from school and encouraged physical exploration. I was trying to expand Chaitanya's horizons and encourage cerebral growth. As parents, we have a responsibility to understand the interests and aptitude of our kids, and create an environment conducive to their growth and excellence. My father and I were both treading the same path.

The joy of receiving a bicycle from my father and giving my son a laptop was similar. The only difference I am able to discern is that of right and responsibility. I hope my son too has begun the process of understanding that the right to receive is married to the responsibility of paying it forward. We all give what we receive. From my father I learnt that investment in education, in self-sufficiency and exploration, is all. I hope Chaitanya learns this too and passes it on.

* * *

Childhood is, or should indeed be, the best phase of our lives. We have the capacity to dispense with worry and care in a way that adulthood simply does not permit. My own childhood was carefree, with very little in the world to bother me. My earliest days were spent in a kuchcha ghar, an uncemented mud and brick structure with no foundation to speak of. Houses like ours figure in narratives of destitution, but I only remember joy. The community we lived in was friendly and our bonds were strong. I had playmates enough for day-long games all day long with. We played all sorts of local and improvised games: pitthoo, kancha, gilli-danda, chuppam-chuppai were regular favourites.

I also liked sports - soccer and cricket - though I never received formal training in either. I also picked up badminton, but it too remained a hobby. During my childhood sports as a viable career option was unheard of. Sports were 'fun and games'; it ended there.

There was no ecosystem to promote sports – neither in the community nor in schools. At my elementary school we only had an annual 'games competition'; it was not even a 'sports meet'. I always won the 100-metre race, but it was no accomplishment. During high school, our Biology teacher taught Physical Education classes. The absence of an extra-curricular infrastructure is, in retrospect, glaringly evident and noteworthy. Our sports 'happened' outside school, in the streets, playing with neighborhood kids. We learned how to organize ourselves into teams, stick to rules, and conduct tournaments.

Going out to play for hours upon hours was routine, but we had no guidance, no direction or intention. What a loss! Sports and co-curricular activities make education holistic and wholesome; institutions that fail to accord them focus, resources or time, hinder their students' growth and progress.

* * *

My formal education started at a Hindi medium school. Well, the elementary school was 'English medium' on paper, but the medium of instruction across all subjects bar English remained Hindi. Thousands of schools across India operate likewise. Such schools cater to parents who want their children to get good education but don't have the wherewithal to send them to wealthier private or boarding schools. They do want a hint of English, the natural companion to success in this country.

My elementary school was perfect in this regard. It had an English name (St Xavier's - though no relation to the missionaries or their group of schools), and a Christian Principal with a Western name. A handful of teachers even knew English. It worked well for my parents, and for many like them.

Our Principal Robert Sir was very 'strict'. If he came ambling down a corridor we would disappear. The teachers were hardworking and demanded like diligence from us. In our day good teachers and principals were known for 'strictness', and for how tough they were on their students. In a way, I suppose, despotism had market value.

The elementary school was not part of any formal board, but it was quite well-structured. My foundation was laid here; I learned the 'fundamental concepts'. I graduated a good, sincere, bright student. At the end of my time in elementary school I had beautiful handwriting, a decent command over English and a passable one over mathematical and scientific concepts for a child my age.

The curriculum had not, however, run parallel with the state board 'syllabus', compromising my transition to secondary school. Additionally, the schools I attended later were explicitly 'Hindi medium': the language of instruction even for English was Hindi!

* * *

My father was very keen to send me outside my hometown for good schooling after the elementary years, but did not know much about schools other than the boarding school my elder brother had been sent to. My brother pronounced the school a bad choice for me. The standards of education in his school had fallen and Sanjay must be sent elsewhere.

There were a few good government schools in Jharkhand, formerly part of Bihar, but I couldn't get through their admissions process. There was a vast difference between what I had learned and what these schools were looking for. The lack of alignment across Bihar's school systems was proving disastrous for me. There was no private higher secondary CBSE (Central Board of Secondary Education) school in my hometown at that time, and no clear path to absorb private school students into government schools, who followed a very different curriculum in a completely different setting.

Many such private elementary schools thrive, not only in Bihar but across the country. The government remains noncommittal about aligning private and government school education. The non-CBSE-affiliated private elementary schools are not accountable to the state, and there are no curricular guidelines or procedures for transitioning students, which leaves them vulnerable.

Like many others, I too was affected by this unplanned system. This early transition is especially challenging; a child cannot fight the system, stand up for the constitutional right to an education, offer solutions, or manoeuver a way through the existing obstacle course. She or he scarcely understands the system's expectations. I secured admission to Harishankar Nayak High School in Katihar, but my father remained dissatisfied with his choice. He wanted to send me out like my brother, so the string of entrances continued till I was admitted to Jhaksu Narayan Chaudhary Boarding High School in Semapur, a closeby village.

* * *

My new school was co-educational but the boarding facilities were for boys only. The Principal, again, was very 'strict' and lived on campus. Although the school routine was like any other government school's, the hostel routine was severe. We had to wake at 5 am and line up for Morning Prayer in the courtyard. Sleepy, groggy or tired, we recited, "Uth jaag musafir bhor bhaye/ab raiin kaha jo sowat hai; jo sowat hai so khowat hai/jo jaagat hai so pawat hai" (arise and awake traveller, dawn breaks/why do you slumber now night is done; they who slumber lose/those who wake gain).

After this 'prayer' we had study hour, sat through in our respective beds. Students swaying with sleep or napping sitting was of the commonest. It was our 'fighting sleep' or 'secretly napping' hour.

For morning ablutions we trudged to fields beyond campus bounds. Open defecation remains common practice, especially in rural India. This was the first opportunity for students to interact without teachers' interference, mediation, or oversight. When we returned we were tasked with cleaning toilets, wiping blackboards, cleaning classrooms, etc., on campus. A team of senior students were designated the responsibility of assigning tasks and they gave easier tasks to their 'favorites'. One of the tasks was to go and give the Principal his morning dose of Ayurveda medicine. Students jockeyed for its ease and for 'exclusive access' to the Principal each morning.

The entire routine was designed to exercise control over students' bodies and natural rhythms, to perpetuate a strictly hierarchical structure and ecosystem.

* * *

While the teachers were academically competent, hostel living remained a sore point for them too. Lack of organization, discipline, and empathy towards the kids was evident. Tasks were left to senior students and resident teachers made arbitrary rules. The senior students laid down more arbitrary rules of their own, became centres of power-by-proxy, and younger pupils expended a good deal of time and effort trying to win favour. Snacks and food from home was a favourite bribe. I used to go home each weekend and pack homemade delicacies for them. Establishing this routine helped me strike close relationships with them as well as a few teachers.

We were given two meals in the hostel – lunch and dinner – without any variation in the menu. Rice and a vegetable was the staple; on Sundays we were served aalu dum and rice. The monotony meant we missed homecooked food terribly and often escaped to local markets for samosas and jalebis. Getting permission from the hostel warden for these samosa-jalebi trips was initially difficult; we had to find a cover-up excuse. Later we developed a good rapport with him and could head out whenever we wanted.

The hostellers had a collective study hour in the evening as well. The roof of the school served as our common study area. We carried a snack, our own kerosene lantern, and books. I cannot really speak for others, but I found this evening exercise quite futile. Students were distracted. Some unabashedly napped away. Teachers did supervise our studies, but students had found ways to escape scrutinizing eyes. Some of them would sit far away as possible from the teacher and read story books and comics, hidden inside textbooks. *Amar Chitra Katha* comics were very popular; *Vikram and Baital*, *Champak*, *Parag*, *Nandan*, and *Chacha Chaudhary* were some of my favorites too.

During my childhood, using sticks and slaps to keep students in line was common practice. Many parents, including my own, preferred teachers with such qualities to inculcate physical discipline: it was part of an 'effective' teacher's skill set.

I was lost amidst rules and schedules, my own identity and freedom were alike elusive, and distraction and disillusionment beckoned. The practice of collective study without any individual attention or focus on individual learning made it easy to feel demotivated, and alienated. I found myself slipping down the academic slope. Hardly any effort was made to stimulate students' interest in learning.

The end was unexpected. After a local boy was denied admission to the school for failing to score high marks on the test, caste-based conflict erupted between the locals and the Principal, affecting the entire school community. It divided the school into two camps. School management were also part of the commotion. The conflict played out at a higher intensity each day and attained its climax when a group of locals attacked the hostel. We, still young and impressionable, witnessed the fight and were naturally frightened and shocked.

It was very painful for me to face the reality of caste distinctions this early in life. Before 7th grade, I think, I had not really grasped this particular societal stratification. Till then, it had been all about class: any family's sole claim to distinction, wealth. I had known that several classmates in my previous school had parents much affluent than mine. But caste? What was that?

I discovered the answer slowly, in JNCBHS. Our senior students found out and told the teachers what castes we belonged to, and thereafter our treatment by teachers and Principal was graded along caste lines. The knowledge alienated me completely.

Six months into my time in Semapur, and it was a winter night. We were settling into our beds when we heard people screaming. Initially we thought perhaps the villagers were shouting at each other. But something was going on very close to our dorm. We came out of the dorm, terrified though we were, to see what was going on. What we saw horrified us even more. There were people with pistols and knives, at least ten or twelve of them, several of whom were drunk. They were abusing the Principal and daring him to come out of house. A few teachers and senior students approached them for calm down and asked them to leave the campus. They were peremptorily attacked. Someone fired his pistol into the air, and we scattered. Ran to our dorms and rooms, where we sat out the night, sleepless, silent and paralysed. Later we learned the Principal had tried to call the police to intervene, but no one showed up. The incursion on the school's peace was left to trickle away on its own. The men left, eventually, but threatened to return and do far more damage: "We will see how you survive here, casteist! You won't admit our ward? Be prepared for the consequences... You think you are safe today? Next time we will kill some of you!"

In an agony of physical fear, we waited for the morning and our Principal's reaction. We were genuinely worried about him. He was known for his commitment to the school and his administrative skill managed to attract students from neighboring districts even though it was located in a village. But he was a Bhumihar, the prospective student was from a backward caste, and in the admissions process he apparently faired poorly. The process itself was anything but transparent.The Principal called a meeting of teachers, held an assembly that informed students of the adults' decision to shut down the school for a while, and helped vacate the hostel. The event seemed godsent. I packed all my stuff, happy to leave, and decided not to come back even if the school reopened. All I had to do to escape with finality was to tell Maa and Babuji the entire story, with all its nearly-gory details.

* * *

Going back to HNHS (Harishankar Nayak High School) would mean I remained in a safe, familiar environment with known faces for company. I did return then, joined the school and the classes and settled in comfortably. In this school there were no boundaries or restrictions. Teachers took classes but students found their own time and ways of having fun.

The Principal of HNHS was a disciplinarian too and kept the school running like clockwork. He personally went on regular 'rounds' to ensure classes were being held on time and students were not loitering aimlessly around campus. Thanks to his efforts and the support of some hard working teachers, HNHS students managed a decent result in the state board exam every year. The school was ranked among the top 5 in the district.

Some of our teachers were extremely knowledgeable, and respected figures to the student fraternity. Our Principal taught too, though he did not take his own classes too seriously. He was an excellent administrator but not a promising teacher. Most days his Economics class, usually during the last hour, was dismissed after a few minutes. "Bhookhe bhaje na hoe gopala," he would say, "the famished cannot recite bhajans." No wonder I never developed much of an interest in Economics!

HNHS was located close to the Officers' Colony, so most of the wards of senior government officials, including the District

Magistrate and District Education Officer, attended our school. In fact the son of the DM and the daughter of the DEO were my classmates. Having them in our batch caused quite a sensation, and was a source of perpetual stress; teachers were under pressure to 'perform'. The school considered it a grave honor to number VIP wards among its students. The sense of privilege also extended to us, who were friends with VIP kids. As a friend of the DM's son I, for instance, got to visit the Collector's Bungalow – my first exposure to such a big, government house. I was fascinated by what I saw – the size, the prestige, the power and the lifestyle which I could never imagine for myself.

One of my special friends regularly got us free passes to the movies since his father was a government officer. My fascination with Bollywood grew exponentially, skipped class to go out, and was thrilled with the imitative potential of stars on screen.

Since HNHS was a government school the student body was quite diverse. Students from all economic classes were present in the school – from kids of washermen to cycle repair person, to sons and daughters of small entrepreneurs and low to high level government officials. This mix benefitted us greatly. I had friends from all walks of life and this interaction helped me a lot in later part of life. I found it easy to adapt in the company of any and every one.

There were no private high schools in town at the time. The sons and daughters of all influential people were, therefore, sent to government schools. The quality of education in these government schools was not bad at all. It was the growing culture of private tuitions which, I believe, led to the rise of private high schools in Bihar in the 1990s. The quality and experience of education in these schools was certainly better as they had more resources at their disposal. Those who could afford the fees certainly sent their children to these private schools instead. Government schools became the resort of the poor, and the exodus of the wealthy and powerful caused a massive deterioration in learning and teaching standards. Once the important stakeholders moved out of their ambit, these schools fell on hard times from which they have yet to recover.

* * *

After my re-entry into the school in the later half of 7th grade, I was able to create a good impression on most of my teachers, including the English literature teacher. All teachers offered private tuitions at home and this was seen as another way to enter their good books. I took up private tuitions for Math, Biology, and English. I struck such a good rapport with my English teacher that two years later he trusted me to mark the final test papers of 7th grade. Regardless of how appropriate and ethical his delegation was, I certainly enjoyed the process immensely. I felt responsible and empowered.

Students are constantly learning, inside the classroom, in the presence of books and teachers, or outside, playing and interacting with friends. I was no exception. In fact, like many, I learned a lot more outside the classroom, in the company of friends and through lived experience, both good and bad. Our classrooms were fairly lacklustre and boring.

Another noteworthy point: though the school was co-educational, boys were not supposed to interact with girls. This was not an explicit, written rule, but an accepted societal norm of the society which we were expected to follow. This was of course also around when we all started becoming conscious of girls and the differences in our social and physical attributes. I, for example, was always unable to understand why boys and girls couldn't sit together or talk together. There was no formal orientation around this reasoning either in the school or in the family. The adolescent boys and girls were left to come to all manner of hormonal conclusions. Traditional gender norms are thus expressed in educational spaces. There were different rows for seating boys and girls. We were not supposed to speak to each other, much less strike up friendships. This exclusionary system made us fetishize girls, engendering curiosity we had no healthy way of satisfying.

I was never very academically inclined. I played a lot of games, but without ambition. I do remember that I encouraged our sports teacher to buy cricket and football kits, and organized classmates to go and buy them from the market. The effort yielded good results – it generated interest in these sports among students. We didn't have a coach; we learned by observing elders and peers play in the railway playground, where cricket and football matches were organized. Some of the cricket idols in town included Bose-da, Bhim, Jaaved, Fahim and Sujeet Singh. Television had still not become popular, so we could only watch amateurs and local professional players actually sweat it out in the ground.

We did not have individually owned sports equipment. We played barefoot since none of us had sneakers or sports shoes. I don't think we were even aware of the importance of correct footwear in helping play a game well. Affordability must have been an issue, but it wasn't distant. We simply didn't know.

Playing cricket was great fun. Our matches were impromptu, with little or no pre-planning. I remember a match that earned me short-lived superstardom among friends. As always, we played an impromptu match at our normal venue – a piece of barren land. Batting first, the rival team had set a big target. Our first batsman was out with a single-figure score. Undaunted, our team put their faith in me and I was pumped enough to take the crease with confidence and a single-minded objective: securing a team win. It was my first and last moment of glory in the cricketing field. My performance consistently fell after that success.

I was a decent badminton player too. I made it to the district finals, but my opponent's stamina defeated me. What I could do best, though, was run. Few runners my age could beat me. But cricket, badminton, or athletics – they remained mere teenage outdoor activities. None of us – my parents, my teachers, or myself – saw any sense in pursuing them professionally. Knowledge of professional sports was too scattered to encourage streamlined effort.

Whenever I cross a village or a small town in India and see kids playing cricket, football, or any other game I get nostalgic. I am also pained at the thought of how many young sporting talents must be languishing in these dust-laden fields, vanishing before they can make their presence felt. India's primary strength is its human resources, yet we have not figured out a way to channelize our talents from villages and small towns. Sports remains restricted to privileged kids.

When I was in 10th grade I met Manish, who became one of the district's most popular cricketers. The son of one of Katihar's leading medical practitioners, he had professional gear – everything, it seemed, one his age could desire. But even a boy as talented and financially stable as him couldn't pursue cricket as a career. It was simply not part of the occupational framework in our town. We heard of a few individuals who pursued sports and got a job in Railways through the sports quota. Nothing more.

I also played table tennis on a chauki, a simple, low, rectangular wooden frame on four legs. The only proper table was available at the Officers Club, where we couldn't, of course, go. So, we had innovated our own little way of enjoying the game: we converted the chauki at Bittu's house into one and played over it. His home was our favorite hang-out.

The beauty of youth is I suppose that nothing seems impossible. Our lives seemed limitless and unconstrained. We charted our own routes to learning, playing, and innovating. Our town was one of limited means and resources, but that did not stop us from having fun. Television didn't enter our lives until 1984, the year Mrs. Gandhi was assassinated. It made rapid inroads into all households thereafter. Wealthier households had colored sets and poorer ones with meagre means could only afford black and white. But even in the absence of knowledge we concocted our own ways of doing things. Table Tennis on chauki is one such example – what is now referred to as 'glocal' – the global game in local style.

* * *

In 9th grade, when I should have been concentrating with vigour on my studies, I made some new 'friends'. Our network of friends usually grew through common friends. At that age we seldom have the ability to assess the impact someone's company can have on us, and conflicts among local groups of young people would escalate into full-blown fist-fights. Such was my fear of being singled out that I sought the protection of a senior because of whom I had already been in one. The old story: for a while I was increasingly trapped in a local gang ecosystem. In return for the assurance of protection, I was supposed to keep his stomach full. Like any petty authority figure he would show up at our small sweet shop and ask for samosas. The entire act was hackneyed extortion, which I escaped with difficulty. Some of my friends and those seniors remained occupied in such activities for years, which wasn't, of course, sustainable for young people that age. So many I thought brilliant and mighty as youngsters failed, dropped out, fell off by the wayside...

But alongside creatures like my private extortionist I also had some wonderful friends, who remain with me to date. We weren't wise enough to help or encourage each other in matters of importance. What kept us glued together was sharing. Whatever we knew or had was for all of us to partake of. Kranti's entry is was erratic who taught me how to ride a motorbike in 9th grade. I didn't have a bike of my own, but Kranti was kind enough to allow all of us to ride it around. For our part, we helped Kranti keep his tank full so he wouldn't get an earful from the family. Most of our friendly activities worked on a cooperative system, of communal use between friends.

Classmates at HNHS also had a great time simply loitering about and visiting our favourite snack vendors for a daily dose of fun. Poddarji bhoonjawala was the most sought after of the lot, and formed a part of our routine. He was a kind man, also popular because he often gave us bhoonja(roasted grains spiced with chopped onions and condiments) on credit if we weren't carrying cash. He knew what variation each of us liked – more, less, or moderate spice. Bhoonja was also a very filling snack during break times.

Our second favourite was the kulfiwala. The chilled kulfi in different flavours was in high demand among students. We vied to pay for each other, And the bonhomie still brings a smile to my face. The whole experience – sharing and paying for everyone – is part of the culture I grew up in. Later in life, of course, when I ventured to Delhi, the Netherlands and the US, I learned how to split the bill and 'Going Dutch' from the term originated in border disputes between England and Holland. I grew comfortable with both the warmth of paying for each other in turn and with the clarity of scrupulously covering one's own costs – but I do not dismiss the value of my childhood lessons in kinship.

* * *

During secondary school I lived a very undisciplined life. Nothing could hold my attention for long – neither studies, nor sports, not even friends. I was looking desperately for something I think, which was not to be found in Katihar. The government school I went to, where I was spending close to forty hours in a week, was insufficient to hold me down. I did not give me enough to expand and satisfy my mind. I used to regularly skip classes, especially after recess, to go to a friend's place and play. All of this came to the family's notice when my elder brother asked me to show him my fee receipt and found that I had paid the palayan dand (post recess disappearance fine). I was interrogated, and the truth came tumbling out of my mouth.

Another practice developed among our gang of friends: we used to hang around at a restaurant called Adarsh in the evening, which was known for its sweets and snacks – especially the samosa. Since we met there frequently, four or five times a week, we developed a good rapport with the owner and his two brothers. They initiated an informal credit system for us. Then, mischief on our minds, we thought of trying something particularly smart. We told one brother that we cleared our account with the other. Since they did not maintain any written records there was no way for them to verify our claim and they took our word for truth. We started enjoying the system – eat samosas and pay for barely any.

We were just youngsters trying to manage on limited pocket money – we certainly didn't consider ourselves habitual offenders then, nor did we grow into irresponsibility or criminality. In fact a few years ago we disclosed this secret to the eldest brother and had a hearty laugh.

* * *

Monsoon. 1986. In grade 9 we were asked by our school whether we wanted to change our name. This was going to be our last chance to do so if we wanted different names on board examination certificates. I had never liked my name. It is commonplace, incapable of lending someone a unique identity. The name, in fact, is so common that I often had to explain to people, "which Sanjay?" when I called them up. I always needed an extra word to complete my identity. I had of course no idea that this name and identity situation was only going to get worse over the years.

I thought long and hard about changing my name, but did not discuss it with my father or mother. I feared they might feel hurt. I did discuss it with my elder sisters - whom I was always more comfortable with than I was with my brothers - but they did not take my desire to change my name seriously. The struggle remained largely internal. Should I change my name? If yes, what should my new name be?

I thought of dozens, most drawn from Bollywood. I wanted to be Kumar Gaurav – the young, fresh, handsome star made famous by *Love Story*, the 'mega hit' film of 1981. I had almost decided upon the name for myself but I couldn't muster up the courage to discuss it with my parents and it remained an unrealized fantasy.

I was disappointed in myself: all this energy I had put into thinking up names and imagining characters went waste. A few kids in my class did change their names and their initiative further saddened me. I still think I missed an important opportunity; I should have changed my name. The feeling is heightened anytime someone asks, "which Sanjay?"

There is more than one side to a circumstance, however. Sanjay means 'even victory'. I share a name with a character in the *Mahabharata*: interpreter to King Dhritarashtra, blessed with divine vision to report the progress of war in the Kurukshetra to the blind and aging king. I can hope that some kind of sight is bestowed on me too, by the virtue of my name, so I can always see beyond obvious reality and make contributions to alleviate our country's socio-economic malaise.

* * *

That year, as my struggle for identity heightened, clothing too became important. What to wear and what not to wear! Unsurprisingly, Bollywood was a significant influence. Looking back I am struck forcefully by the fact I never discussed any of my adolescent preoccupations with elders, and they never commented on the fragility or the vulnerability of being young – or the consequences of my choices. Bollywood stars inspired me, but they were inimitable to me, for two reasons – I could neither afford their garments, nor did I have the 'natural style' or carriage to pull them off. Still, we did make few day trips to Biratnagar in Nepal, where all these fancy clothes could be procured at very cheap prices.

* * *

What I have meant to convey is that growing up in Katihar was fun. I did not gain much of a formal education, but I did gain some solid practical and social exposure. I made some friends to keep and broke away from some. I played a lot of 'games'. I learned many life skills –how to interact with a diverse set of people in different and sometimes difficult situations. I innovated. I struggled with my identity. My childhood, like everyone's, had a deep impact on what I would become over the following years. The foundation was laid, even if I had scant comprehension of it. What remained to be seen is what structure I would hereon build.

❑❑

Chapter Three

Failure

One ordinary Sunday afternoon as I was sitting down with my son Chaitanya and describing what we would do during an upcoming vacation. He asked me, "Papa, where all did you go on vacation when you were a child?" The question caught me off guard. After a brief moment I answered, "To our village." He was confused. Did he imagine beaches and mountains in my vacation plans?

"Didn't you ever go outside Bihar for a holiday?" I replied in the negative. He was quiet for a while.

"So, when did you first step outside Bihar?" The question sent me many, many years back, reliving times and situations that had propelled me out of Katihar to explore the world, for the first time, on my own. Memories that were at once simple and complex, sweet and painful.

I left my hometown, and Bihar, for the first time at the age of fifteen in 1987.

One sultry July Babuji booked a berth in the second-class sleeper of the North-East Express. I was undertaking this journey alone, and the circumstances churned a complex mix of anxiety and excitement in me. I had no idea what Delhi was going to be like. Other than the short, disappointing stint at the residential school just outside Katihar I had not ventured out at all. And now

I leaving behind not only my town, but my entire state! This was going to be one hell of a journey.

Arbind bhaiya was waiting for me at the Delhi station. The city was swarming with people. To say I was overwhelmed when I saw the infinite mass of people, all pushing and pulling and making a way for themselves, would be an understatement. I was astonished we managed to get out, and take an autorickshaw to my brother's hostel in Delhi University. I was in an alien land, but before any discomfort could settle in my body and mind, my brother's friends took it upon themselves to put me at ease.

I was in North Campus. For a few days I stayed with my brother in his hostel at Hindu College. Delhi was 'the city of opportunities' and my brother tried his best to make me understand the importance of being here, and also to pump me full of zeal and the confidence to make good use of my time here. I was looking forward to it, but nothing had prepared me for the kind of melting pot experience Delhi had in store for me. The city gave me tremendous exposure, but I kept losing my grip on schoolwork. Education was a perpetually slippery slope.

I was in no way a 'serious' student during my high school days. Life would exact a heavy price for this lackadaisical attitude. My friends and frolicking with them figured far higher on my list of priorities than reading, or developing an interest in studies. I was directionless.

Like most families with our socio-economic baggage, mine too wanted me to pursue medicine as a career. My father neither had any opportunity nor resources for such a dream. But he dreamed for his children. We were 6 in all – 3 sons and 3 daughters. I was the fifth child born to my parents. Arbind bhaiya had also been encouraged to study medicine but he had read Social Sciences at university. Arun bhaiya, my eldest brother, was inspired by the JP movement and held his social responsibilities in rather higher regard than familial ties and expectations. Any doors of speculation on his choices and careers were thus shut firmly. Anita didi was also clear she wanted to Study Social sciences. Rita didi, because she was bright and did well in science classes from early on, became the one expected to fulfil our parents' aspirations.

She was sent to Patna for Medical Entrance Test coaching classes. She worked very hard, but finally couldn't qualify for admission to medical schools. It was a difficult time for her, but I was more concerned on my own account! The burden of expectations left unfulfilled by her and my other older siblings was now pushed onto me.

Today we are expected to groom our children for self-awareness, self-reliance, and to be assertive. We expect them to choose their own career paths and see ourselves as facilitators and mentors along their path. This was not the case till quite recently. The family's collective will had more weight than the individual's aspirations, even if family expectations were contrary to the child's capacities. The child was seldom asked for an opinion or for preferences. And this seeming anachronism does still persist. Many families still overrule individual desires, leading to unfulfilled personal and professional lives. It does strike me as absurd how little is invested in understanding the child's natural abilities and nurturing them: surely that would be maximally productive? The weight of the family dream onto my shoulders, for instance, proved disastrous for me. I was a decent student through elementary and middle school, but lost the plot in high school. And though I failed to keep up in most classes, it was science that slipped my grasp completely. Yet I was asked not only to continue studying it after high school, but to carve a career in a science-driven field.

With average grades in hand, I couldn't get through any good school in Delhi for admission to grade eleven. A series of underwhelming and confidence-scarring incidents later I landed in a government school in Rana Pratap Bagh, North Delhi. Located in a neighbourhood called C.C. Colony, it seemed like a cradle for subpar performers.

The school itself was uninspiring, insipid, and decidedly disappointing to hopes from the great city of Delhi. But what choice did I have? I was not going back home. The fees were reasonable since it was a government school, and affordable for my folks. My parents proudly informed all and sundry that their son had gone to study in Delhi; where I was actually studying did not merit particular comment. The transition to a new city, a new school, a new system of learning, framed by a different educational board (CBSE), was not easy. Each day was an exercise in coping.

Then, my new school in the National Capital Region was not just dull, it suffered tremendously from institutional gaps. The core of any teaching-learning experience is the teacher. They say a school is only as good as its teachers – this community of professionals has near-miraculous wherewithal to shape and transform generations. The painful truth, however, is that the profession and its development have been disregarded abysmally by successive governments. Private institutions have been permitted to exploit their staff, lowering the value of 'teaching' and 'teachers' in society. Ambitious and capable citizens rarely take up the profession - and those who do are habitually disparaged. It is no wonder that most government schools in our country suffer from an abominable paucity of good teachers. Instead of nurturing their pupils, many of them are apathetic towards welfare as well as pedagogy, doing great disservice to the entire concept of education. They cannot build holistic personalities, capable of responsibly taking the future of the world in their hands.

My school was typical. Teachers were absent. They lacked inspiration. They were at best dispassionate about their chosen field of study, and consequently not very good at what they were teaching. They saw no need to encourage or support students, and seldom paid attention to distresses flinging down roots in us. Their engagement in class was negligible; they did not care to associate with us outside class at all. I do not recall a single mentor figure among them. And the result? Careless and directionless students succumbing to self-destruction. The school environment was suffocatingly boring, and students found dark avenues of entertainment, which included but was not limited to the distribution of pornography and widespread substance abuse.

If the insides of the classrooms were dull, co-curricular activities and attention toward the development of children's personalities were non-existent. Stepping into school every morning added no value to anyone's day. I did not want to go there. I did not want to meet my fellow students; they disgusted and further demotivated me. There was no teacher I looked forward to seeing or learning from. I felt I deserved better but my poor grades meant I was destined to suffer.

I was choking and no one knew it.

The mind of a young student has been likened to soil, which can be made fertile only through adequate nutrition and nourishment. The nourished youthful mind is a fecund environment where revolutionary ideas for tomorrow can take root and blossom into lush plants to feed the future. If you withdraw light and nutrients from the same soil, however, it will become barren and crumble into grains of dust which can only be blown about aimlessly.

I was sinking. As an individual and as a student. I stopped challenging myself. I did not feel like pushing myself or hope for anything positive from my life. I felt stuck between the pride of my family and the morose reality of my school environment. The last and final straw for my plummeting spirit was this new city and its demanding lifestyles.

Delhi was an expensive city to live in. Of modest origin, I could hardly afford anything other than the bare minimum of survival. My expenses were set in stone– rent for a shared room, money for simple meals and transport allowance. By this time I was living in Jawahar Nagar, near Kamla Nagar, close to the North Campus. Bread and jam was my staple breakfast for two years and lunch comprised chholey-chawal at a corner hawker in Shakti Nagar. Dinner mostly at a dhaba near Malka Ganj with four tandoori rotis and a sabzi. Life droned on. Nothing moved. Nothing changed. I felt I was passing time without any growth. That I was moving backward.

Adolescence is crucial. You build your personality (social, emotional, and physical), and start charting a course for the future. And here I was, losing both years and hope, as well of course as opportunities. The pace of life, which had slowed down during my last years in Katihar was just not willing to pick up, even in the seemingly fast-paced metropolis.

* * *

My parents and my elder brother, Arbind bhaiya, my support structure, had no inkling of all this. We were distanced by age and space, and there was no culture of sharing and interaction at this level. We were close, and attached to each other, but I don't remember having any conversations on issues of critical importance with people in my family, as if this discourse was somehow prohibited. Lack of communication within families is debilitating, but it is rampant.

My exam performance was dismal. Still, this did not raise the requisite alarms. I couldn't prepare well for the twelfth Boards and, unsurprisingly in retrospect, I failed. This time, literally.

The world came crashing around me. I couldn't believe it. I couldn't believe I could fail an exam. I had shamed not just myself, but my whole family. I was scared to face my parents and my brother. This fear was real, physical, and it crippled my body and my mind for several days. What will I do now? Where will I go from here? I was shattered. And so were any final remnants of my self-confidence.

❑❑

Chapter Four

The Turnaround

I went to see my family after the results came out. In my head, I carried the tag of a loser. I didn't know how to face them. I didn't know what to say. Then I realized I didn't have to say anything. The whisper network in small towns is formidable. News of my failure had reached everyone and I could see it staring back at me through the silence in their eyes.

Failure, this personal failure, entitled an army of friends and relatives to have a say in my life. "Why don't you send him to Calcutta? I know someone there who can help him become a private security guard," advised a well-wisher. Money for him, in the profession was good and there was going to be a great demand for security personnel in the coming years. "Why don't you make Sanjay apply for a clerical job in Railways? I'll be happy to help," chimed in another good samaritan. Both of them, and everyone else, meant well. Genuinely well. But their well meaning visions, which limited the scope of my possible futures, made me question my own worth in a serious way.

I couldn't remain silent. I had to speak with my father. I had failed him again, and I didn't know what he would say. Approaching him, standing in front of him, facing him – I was overwrought. I must have been on the verge of a breakdown when I saw the expressions on my father's face. There was no trace of anger. He must have felt bad, but he did not display any anger. I sighed with relief.

I decided to stay back in Katihar and support him. I wanted to give up my studies and continue living in my hometown. This wasn't a sacrifice, it seemed like the easy thing to do. I had turned into an escapist – rather than face my failures and set things right, I had decided to run away, duck my head and firmly shut my eyes to memories of failures and the need for proving myself. Being in Katihar and doing odd-jobs also saved me from studying Science. I was in fact being a coward and needed to be called out. Arbind bhaiya proved the messiah to accomplish this harsh but important task.

When he asked me what I planned to do now, I simply stated my desire to stay back and help Babuji. "Sanjay, if you really want to help Babuji, you have to study, remember?" came his pat reply. It sort of closed all need for further conversation. My brother understood that I was scared and he counseled me, but he also jolted me out of complacence, and made me understand that in life, there are no easy ways out.

* * *

I had to build everything again. I had to clear the higher secondary exam to have a shot at further education. I did not want to take any more risks. My biggest failure, as so often happens, was my greatest teacher.

I prepared tirelessly. I had lost my self-confidence and Delhi had lost it charm. It made sense to come back to Katihar and dive into study. My parents were happy with my decision. They were, in fact, keen to not leave me alone at such a crucial phase in life. From CBSE I went back to the Bihar Intermediate Education Council, and gave it my all.

My diligence paid off. I scored a little over 60 percent, clearing the exams in 1991 with the dignity of a first division. The greatest surprise was that I scored well in the Sciences too! Of course after this I never took up Science and Math again, and this I do regard as the collective failure of our institutional frameworks. I also think it imperative schools, families, and societies counsel the young, and then let them follow their own path, because while successes are owned by many, failure is thrust onto just one body. I was the sole recipient of all blame for all implications of my poor performance. I was robbed of two years of life with a total of four years then spent in constant struggle, to 'succeed'. I felt responsible for a mountainous mess and that I had to work hard to clear this blot off my name. I did manage it all in the end, and could move on in life, but I think incessantly of the many, many who can't. Failure must not be made doubly debilitating.

* * *

What Delhi *had* taught me was that there was a life beyond Katihar. This life, clearly, demanded ruthless hard work, which was also necessary to avoid the fate of becoming a railway clerk or a private security guard. I do not mean to disparage these occupations, to suggest they lack dignity or are unimportant. But they were *familiar*. My germinating aspirations asked me to seek beyond these known pastures.

The strangest situations empower us with the strongest resolves. I had never braved my way into a Delhi restaurant. The limited monthly monetary support from my father prohibited all such indulgences. However, my cousin Ramesh bhaiya and my flatmates Gokulda, Bittu, and Vighnesh once insisted that we go to the newly opened Miglani Restaurant in Indra Vihar. Reluctantly, I went. After serving us water the waiter gave us the menu card. One glance and we realized a meal here would leave us starving through the month. We decided to walk out immediately. As we did, a burden seemed to settle on my heart, that resembled shame. I don't exactly know what I was ashamed about, but I resolved never to be in such a situation again. I needed to earn money, I needed to do well in life, I needed to start working very, very hard.

* * *

The 60 percent in my higher secondary exam would just secure admission in Satyawati's Evening College. Life couldn't suddenly become a fairy tale, but it was moving ahead, one step at a time. Satyawati was by no means reckoned among the top colleges of Delhi, but with my baggage of constant disappoints, being able to study in Delhi University at all was a huge consolation.

I picked Political Science as my field. The physical sciences were out of question. My brother and his friends were pursuing History, Political Science, and Sociology. These subjects found favor among many students from Bihar, who were on a mission to crack the civil services exam. History was the most popular subject for this cohort, but I couldn't see myself memorizing dates and events. Sociology and Anthropology were available only in a few colleges. I made my choice, and felt wise. Destiny could have easily shut its doors on me, but here it was, giving me another chance, and I had to make use of it. This time, I had to prove my mettle.

I wanted to learn with a hunger which had not assailed my being before in life. Knowledge had become the means and the end. My elder brother requested the professors at Hindu College to let me attend their classes, and they agreed. I studied there throughout the year and enjoyed the time spent inside lecture rooms tremendously. The teachers were nice and well-versed with their subjects. It is amazing what an impact passionate and informed teachers can have on their students. I was following my teachers' lectures; I found I loved the experience of being a student at the university! Political Science, it seemed, evoked deep interest in me. I began reading prescribed and recommended books independently. Diving into concepts and discussing them with peers became a habit. Finding applications of learnt concepts in the real world also became important. I started observing closely the role of judiciary and the government, while comparing our government machinery with that of other countries. There was great fascination in equating the textual world with the lived world. This link between what we were learning and what we were living had been missing till this point. Here is where I found great joy and finally began liking academics.

I felt a different person. There was a sudden and drastic change in my thought process, my affinity for learning and my entire outlook on living. My failures had made me sincere. I started valuing my time. I avoided all distractions and interactions which added no value to my life. I vowed not fall into any trap which might derail me just as I was picking up steam.

I was attending college at two places – Satyawati and Hindu– but the situation did not pose much of a conflict since my Satyawati classes were scheduled for evening. My batchmates at both the colleges were supportive. In fact at Hindu College I was so well integrated into the class that I took part in almost every discussion and planned class activity. I did attempt to maintain a low profile, but that only served to deepen my focus on study. I was also immensely proud of the fact that some of the best professors, who had authored important books and research papers, were my gurus now. Well-known and well-regarded names like K. K. Mishra and Satya Rai were teaching me. It was a rare privilege and constant motivation.

North Campus is a unique niche in the city of Delhi. Anyone who has been there cannot help but notice its distinct culture, influenced by students coming from all over India. There is a sobriety in the air, leaning towards academic and intellectual discourse. At the same time there is an alacrity to the intermingling of plural thought and culture, leading to a very diverse ecosystem. It was fascinating to be in such a space!

This is not to idealize DU. Colleges afforded much freedom to students who, at the fag end of their adolescence, had a proclivity for trying out new things, not all which were good for them. They did not yet appreciate that freedom needs to be used responsibly. Too many also did not understand that this was among the most crucial periods of their lives, the dividends of which would suffuse their futures. College life is equated with fun that's how we see it in pop culture representations as well. But I had no time to lose.

* * *

After a year of pleasant indulgence in study, it was exam time. I liked my subject, and had consistently prepared notes and kept myself informed. My seniors at the University had also been kind and supportive, doling out advices during examinations. I was confident of doing well, but nervousness constantly assaulted me. I had given these exams my all, but the demons of past disappointments were not easy to vanquish. Mustering courage, pulling together every last drop of confidence, and investing every second to diligent revision, I appeared for the papers and left the rest to the Almighty.

* * *

The day of the result. My heart was thumping and my palms were soaked in sweat. Was the past going to repeat itself? Would I be able to remain afloat this time? Thoughts raged and rallied in all directions. Finally, I collected myself and opened my eyes.

I had stood first in class!

I didn't even know how to react to such news. It was a completely new feeling, a different experience, a strange turn of affairs. To call myself happy would be beside the point: I had become my own little star. I had risen in my own eyes.

I had scored 58.5 percent, slightly short of first division, but in the days before grade inflation that was the highest scored by anyone in my class. Everyone congratulated me. I received dozens of compliments. I was riding high, but the thought of my family, especially of my brother, kept me grounded too. I had made them proud for a moment but my focus could not waver, now. I was the underdog who had proven himself, but there could be no looking back.

Within a year, life completely transformed. This one success motivated me to aim higher. Or rather, for the highest.

In line with tradition, the college awarded me with a trophy and a certificate by the Union Human Resource Minister Murli Manohar Joshi during the Annual Day. This was my first public recognition. The moment my name was announced as the top scorer in Political Science is forever sealed in my trove of special memories. The incredulity of the situation remained, but the fervor to continue the journey uphill kept getting stronger.

* * *

The University had a provision under which a student could transfer to a better college if he or she scored well. I saw my academic achievement as an opportunity to formally study at

Hindu College, and so applied for a transfer there. Unfortunately, however, owing to a large class size, Hindu had decided against taking any new students. When the Principal of Satyawati College heard about my request for transfer and the subsequent refusal, he called me to his office and said, "It is alright. Don't switch colleges. It is better to rule in hell than to serve in heaven." This thought, however strange in the circumstances, did work as consolation. Life continued apace and we were into our second year of study.

* * *

My academic performance during our first year had also earned me respect among my bachelortte at Hindu College. Out of eighty five students at Hindu, only ten or so had scored better. I got a secret high from having matched up, and marched ahead of those so far ahead a year ago.

We all had the same opportunities, the same access to teachers and to study material. What differed was individual effort and motivation. For many, getting into Hindu College itself was an end. What followed did not merit effort or attention. My notion of success, however, was different. Not having bagged the brand name, college was purely a medium to study well, get good grades, and gain knowledge. Many were blinded by freedom and privilege; I understood the cost of both. My quest for excellence continued, academic and personal.

My little academic victory had granted me popularity. Not just Satyawati and Hindu - students from other colleges also started recognizing me. I was consulted, and great value was placed on my notes. My suggestions were taken seriously and the respect which came along with these interactions made my confidence swell.

There were some students at Hindu, mainly from my own home state of Bihar, who refused to look at me as anything other than a lowly student from Satyawati. Some expressed shock at my grades, now higher than theirs. They seemed outraged that previous success did not guarantee future victory. Now that I had a level playing field, I had made good use of the opportunity I had been granted, outgrowing or avoiding the sense of complacency which had taken root in them. There is no shortcut to success.

Hard work, consistency, and commitment: these are indispensable in a student's life.

* * *

I continued doing well. Second year was more fun now that I had completely 'owned' Political Science. We were engaged in comparative political analyses and I really enjoyed learning about different models of governance while gaining an insight into our own political systems. Classrooms were alive with debates and discussions. My mind brimmed with theories and thoughts, and though it was easy to get carried away by intellectual discourse, I kept reminding myself that there was homework to be done each day, lest this intellectual engagement go waste.

I continued the same pattern of study – followed the word of teachers in the class, read the text and some additional material, and then borrowed notes from seniors to further supplement my understanding. This is also when I picked up the habit of reading newspapers, supremely helpful to a Political Science student. All this converged in my own notes, which I diligently prepared on each topic. Since I had now fallen into a rhythm, second year felt easier. Following the basics, I had my formula for doing well in exams. And my scored soared even higher – I attained 61.5 percent.

I had expected it this time. I was rational enough to understand that the Almighty neither miraculously granted you good scores, nor failed you in divine spite. So while I battled huge uncertainty before first-year results, I was relaxed now. My estimate was precise. The second year result helped me understand a few things about myself. First, I was on the right track. Second, I had the potential to do better than other, supposedly better, fellow-students. Third, failures don't go in vain. And finally, nothing in life is permanent – neither the highs, nor the lows. Time changes, and so do we.

* * *

Having conquered the proverbial battlefield in the first two years, it was now time to also have some fun. In the third year, as my confidence in myself was resuscitated, I would give myself time off to watch films with friends. It served as a great stressbuster during exams. The other fun activity we indulged in was taking a full circle of the Ring Road in the Mudrika bus. Being a college student afforded us some privilege: we got a student bus pass for a mere 12.50 rupees, and we made sure we used it well. With friends, or alone, a drive along the Ring Road was therapeutic, and we would see the varied shades of Delhi passing right in front of our eyes.

* * *

In the third year, I scored 59.5 percent, a tiny bit short of first division. This left me greatly dissatisfied, because now the average of all three years was down to under 60 percent too. There were only fifteen first divisions in Political Science throughout the University, and ought to be ranked among them. I challenged my result. After an excruciating wait of three months, I was awarded with a 0.5 percent increase, correcting a miscalculation in my Political Thought paper. I was in the exclusive club of first division holders, and on cloud nine.

* * *

The three years in the University compensated for everything that had happened before them. My turnaround was real. You could see it in the results. You could see it in my personality. You could also see it in the beliefs I had built for my future. I felt the distinct joy of finally leaving darkness behind. I was no longer suffering the pain of having brought shame to my family. I did not appreciate the repercussions of my successes and failures on my parents, but now, a parent myself, I know exactly how fiercely they must have felt them.

Three consecutive years of success made me stronger. The critics had been silenced, and some had turned into admirers. They had no comments to made, except that they had always known I had it in me, that I was a naturally talented boy. I cannot help laughing whenever I remember their comments.

I resumed contact with everyone, and came out of the self-imposed isolation. The sense of failure and the shame associated with it had ebbed away. I was happy. I was social. I was back!

❑❑

Chapter Five

Disillusionment and Rediscovery

1982. When I was about to turn 9, I felt the need to invite all my friends home and throw a party. It had never been a tradition in my home, but some of my friends celebrated their birthdays with much fun and fanfare. I found the idea attractive.

With much hesitation, I tip-toed over to the joint guardians of the household cornucopia – Maa and her assistants, my three sisters. They agreed, but said that while they could cook nice food for my friends, getting a cake was out of question. My face must have fallen a little, because what is a birthday without a celebratory cake? So they made me a 'halwa cake'! So I did get to cut a cake, albeit in its desi avatar. Living with limited means makes you adept at finding alternatives, and you don't really bother too long about things beyond your means.

This practice of keeping in sync with one's background and reality has been part of my earliest years. Growing up nurtured it further. I saw affluence all around me in DU, but I was never really affected by it. I enjoyed with my friends, but knew when to call it a day or where to draw the line.

Delhi University was a parallel world. North Campus was a fascinating island, which had much to offer. From the sincerity of attending lectures to the fun of skipping classes, from the humble tea stall conversations to splurging in upmarket cafes, from the rigour of sports to artistic expression in the form of theatre, dance, and music, from hanging out with friends to romancing in quiet corners – it had something for everybody. Within a ten kilometer radius lay ensconced a vibrant diversity.

I had a string of 'first time' experiences during my time at the University. I tasted my first Kwality ice-cream. I bought my first Snow White branded pullover from Kamla Nagar. I topped my class for the first time. I began preparing my breakfast myself for the first time. And I started taking tuitions to supplement my monthly pocket money for the first time. University life was making me independent, responsible, and self-reliant.

I also explored many areas hitherto unknown to me. Student politics, organising fests and events, parties and celebrations and culinary skills – all were a new addition to my list of experiences. I made some good friends during this period, a few became constant and firm presences through all seasons of life.

Friends have their own unique importance. What begins as a fun association often transforms into relationships which challenge you, support you, and that help expand your worldview. Their perspectives add to your own. Their homes become your comfort zones. One such friend was Subrat. He lived in Surya Nagar in Ghaziabad, and we had started treating his place like a second home. His mother and elder sister, Alka didi, took care of us as though we were their own. We ate, enjoyed, and went on several nights out. In fact, Subrat's Maruti 800 was the first car I rode in, and it became a regular mode of transport for to visiting his place. For the small town boy in me, all these were alien experiences.

In our time campus life was segregated into pockets based on the social, economic and educational backgrounds of students. Despite these boundaries, opportunities were democratic and equally available to all. One of my elder brother's friends used to often say of undergrad years were the "honeymoon period" of a student's life. It's true. While we had our share of fun during the undergrad years, a natural sobriety set in once our Master's programs began.

* * *

In fact, after college life itself acquired a serious hue. Trepidation about careers and our professional futures started looming large in front of our eyes. Each one of us was set to follow a different course. Some chose the management field, others decided to remain in academia. My aim at the time was to become a civil servant, and this demanded more time to study and prepare.

The preparation conflicted with Master's study. Since I wanted to do my post-graduation in Political Science, I decided to enrol in DU itself. I was hoping for another two years where the romance of learning would continue unabated, but I was in for an unpleasant surprise. The Master's program was a dull and unsatisfying experience. To begin with, the syllabus seemed irrelevant and not in sync with evolving times. Our teachers were good and well-known names in the field, but classes were irregular and inadequate to nourish our hungry brains. Students didn't mind the irregularity because most of them had other commitments – like preparation for competitive exams. The arbitrariness suited them. I am not sure these creases have yet been ironed out. My time was definitely unfulfilling, academically speaking.

This period also presented a rude shock with respect to campus life. I was living in Mansarovar Hostel in North Campus, and it was here that caste divisions started revealing their ugly face. PG students, especially North Indians, were firmly divided along caste lines and imposed caste hierarchies among students. Many teachers too reinforced this framework.

In campus, caste favoured caste; merit, qualifications, and other considerations were conveniently ruled out. The selection process for getting a hostel seat was tough and well-defined; but the caste gurus had worked out mechanisms to help and favour those they considered their own. Hostels and wardens had also acquired a reputation for accommodating only particular castes. This practice extended beyond DU, I had heard. Caste was hardwired into academia - and nothing could disappoint me more. Was academia fulfilling its purported goals at all? Was education any good if it could not help the young rise above regressive structures and practices?

I too was exposed to this caste segregation. The Mansarovar Hostel president was a supporter and promoter of caste loyalty. He kept a coterie of students around him, fellow caste-mates. He once called three students of the same caste and handed them a list of applicants to the hostel. I was one among those. Our task was to sort out the names of people of our own caste for selection and put the others aside. He was sure that once we had selected the names he would figure out a way to get them into the hostel. The entire exercise seemed regressive, ridiculous and nonsensical - of course I refused to play any part in it. Names and titles were in any case insufficient to figure out who belonged to which caste! It seemed to me that he was more concerned with puffing himself and his underlings up at the cost of whatever social and political camaraderie might be possible in a communal educational space than even the misplaced 'loyalty' he framed it as.

Because the interesting thing is that even for the hardliners, caste affiliation did not necessarily or automatically mean loyalty at all. The younger brother of the same president was assaulted by one of the students he had had admitted to the hostel. Caste was a social drama, a shallow structure of belonging that stopped students from seeing each other as individuals with qualities, merits, imperfections, and impeded natural associations between them. Above all, it was a gross deviation from the primary aim – knowledge production. The absolute lack of cognizance among younger students that the seasoned caste goons were merely serving their own agenda while playing one group off against another was especially disheartening. No one stood to gain from such a system except the thuggish leaders, who won political currency through their ugly actions. Mansarovar was not the only hostel affected by caste politics; Jubeilee Hall, Gwyer Hall, and others were affected too.

* * *

Caste was huge, but it wasn't the only ill. Students from my hostel spent hours discussing 'girls' from nearby Khalsa College, ruining any opportunities for the development of sensitivity to gender issues so urgent in coeducational spaces inhabited by the young, or any semblance of healthy relationships between women and men. Even food was annexed for power games. A veritable food nexus operated in DU hostels, with command over the kitchen and dining hall spots; there was preferential treatment at meals, and extra portions denied to the 'commoners'. An urban feudal system was in place in our hostels, with the overlords ruling our daily routine and everyday rituals.

Where did this leave me? In a very difficult place, again. The importance of a stimulating, enabling environment in the life of a student cannot be emphasized enough. My grades plummeted again. Alone in the city, I really needed an infrastructure of support. The life I was living in the hostel, though, was not conducive to its creation. It was a dark den of shenanigans which I could never bring myself to explore with aplomb. In the two years I spent at the hostel, I neither progressed in my subject nor succeeded in preparing for the civil services exams. As soon as I thought I could, I decided to leave the hostel.

The charm of DU had worn off.

* * *

My cousin - with whom I had attempted Miglani restaurant - was a student at Jawaharlal Nehru University. I decided to try my luck. I gave the entrance test in 1997 and was admitted to the M. Phil./ Ph. D. program in the South Asian Studies division at the School of International Studies. Besides my M. Phil. course work, I also started preparing for the civil services exam again.

There is a limit to the attempts for civil services; each attempt is precious. JNU was full of students aspiring to be future IAS, IFS, and IPS officers, so, little coaching hubs had mushroomed around campus. Study material and guidance was amply available. Planted back into an invigorating, studious environment, the learner in me throve again.

My Political Science background helped me a lot in M. Phil., especially for the papers on International Politics. During the second year, we were supposed to write a dissertation, and I decided to write mine on what was called 'women's issues'. My supervisor was keen to know why a man wished to research 'women's issues'. Only female students were usually inclined to work on them. That was in fact precisely my motivation. Men needed to work on women's issues, and to be seen doing so. I said so. I was granted permission after a few intense rounds of discussion, and wrote my dissertation on perspectives and policy alternatives in Bangladeshi women's development. The process was unbelievably enriching, though I little knew then just how useful all my research would soon be, when I got down on the ground to work with women on solving their 'issues'.

* * *

My M. Phil. / Ph. D. supervisor Professor I. N. Mukherji, was an accomplished academician, a meticulous guide, and a kind human being. He challenged my capacities as a student, but also made me feel comfortable. In no time, it seemed, we had developed an excellent rapport. He was particular about work, always pushing me to improve my research skills as well as my language and my writing ability. He did not shy away from giving me an earful when my work was not up to par, but also took great pains to guide me personally. He was an affable Bengali, always available for his students and liberal with sweets when we visited his residence.

Professor Muchkund Dubey, ex-Foreign Secretary in the government of India was also among my teachers at JNU. He was very disciplined and demanded rigour from all of us. He was animated, passionate, and fascinating inside the classroom, and if he ever observed a student had been missing his classes, he wouldn't shy away from pursuing the student outside class and demanding explanations. His classes were memorable too for all the personal anecdotes he related, about his government assignments, his foreign trips, and his practical experience – none of which could ever be bound between the covers of a textbook.

Among other wonderful teachers were Professor Kalim Bahadur and Professor S. D. Muni. While the former was an authority on Indo-Pak relations, the latter was known for his expertise in Strategic Affairs.

With such a luminous set of mentors, I was learning with verve again. International Affairs, specially South Asian studies, became my favourite topic of engagement. In a class test conducted by Professor Muni, I was one of only two students to 'understand' his question (the other, Vijoo Krishnan, went onto become the JNU student body President and do good things after university as well). The fact that most of the class had failed to grasp his question - failed to engage with it - upset Professor Muni profoundly. The point, he said, was simple – if the teachers were putting in exceptional effort to stretch our capacities and minds, nothing less than an equal and reciprocal response was expected from us. It was the first time I thought seriously about dedication in the teaching profession, and the impression went a long way to helping me begin putting the dismal last DU years behind, and regain a course that took study as pivot in my life.

* * *

Other than classroom instruction, JNU regularly organized seminars and lectures to supplement our understanding and open more channels of thought and debate among us. Experts, commentators and academic stalwarts were regularly invited to these seminars and we were given the opportunity to directly engage with them.

In these lectures, I came face to face with people I had only ever read about in newspapers. Prominent international strategic affairs analyst, journalist, and former civil servant K. Subramanyam, and former journalist H. K. Dua are among speakers I remember most from our departmental seminars. Many diplomats also marked their presence in these lectures, making our sojourn at the School of International Studies even more dynamic and exciting. Policies and their implementation became my primary areas of interest.

Life in JNU was very different from that in DU. For one thing the physical boundary of the two campuses were very different. JNU was, in the proper sense, a campus with a clearly defined premises. DU was an open city space with innumerable entry and exit points. Living on the JNU campus was monetarily affordable, with many dhabas offering great food at very low prices. Campus life extended into the wee hours of night; in fact, one wondered if the campus ever actually slept.

JNU was also a very politically active space. One became politically aware even through participation in common dhaba discourse. During student elections, issues from both within and outside campus were widely discussed. So in one breath we would be talking of the Gulf War and in the other, of hygiene and sanitation on campus. But as in DU's caste coeteries, hypocrisies took root even within this very woke and aware atmosphere. Student leaders vociferously enunciating the ills of globalization who would drink only foreign liquor and used multinational branded mobile phones were hard to take seriously. And of course though issues were raised, they were rarely if ever settled effectively.

* * *

Another milestone: computers were introduced to JNU during our time. We had a separate computer center, which introduced and trained us to use these machines of the future. Later, each school got a few dedicated systems of its own. We were required to book slots for using computers and accessing the web. Connectivity was excruciatingly slow; a twenty-first century child would kick their system in frustration if they were teleported to our time and place then. Of a thirty minute slot, fifteen minutes were spent waiting to get connected! But though the internet was a test of patience and far from instantly gratifying by today's standards, it was fun to be 'online'. The experience was novel; it was like being given a new toy. We learned the basics, and waited for the payoff in faster, more fortunate times.

The year before I finished my M. Phil., I also appeared for the Civil Services prelims, and cleared the exam. Though the preparation required for the subsequent 'mains' was vast and rigorous, and coupled with my M. Phil. work the task seemed nigh impossible, I scored well there too. I began preparing for the next round. And then suddenly life switched tracks, abruptly.

A senior member of SEWA (Self-Employed Women's Association) approached me to join them. SEWA is a women-centric, grassroots organization. My elder brother was working as Coordinator for a network of street vendors organizations named NASVI (National Association of Street Vendors of India) and SEWA was a key collaborator. I had attended one of their regional workshops in Delhi, and been introduced to a few leaders from SEWA. Since SEWA was keen to expand their efforts in Delhi, they thought I might be interested in working with them for a while.

I had no interest in joining an NGO (Non Governmental Organization). I was besotted with the common national ambition – especially for students from Bihar – that of becoming a civil servant. Also, both my elder brothers were working with NGOs in Bihar. There was no question of a third one following the same course.

I refused the proposal. I was approached again, this time with the request for taking on a seven month task of organizing Gujarati women street vendors into Self-Help Groups and helping find a female candidate for expanding SEWA's work in Delhi. I felt bad, but again said 'No'. After my many failures and the turnaround, I did not want to take any risks. I was neck-deep in UPSC (Union Public Service Commission) prep and did not want to take up anything that might distract me. I was approached a third time. I gave in. It occurred to me that I had, after all, no work-experience behind me. Perhaps I was being precious. I also thought that if this opportunity was knocking at my door again and again, I probably ought to embrace it; perhaps it was meant to be.

This hesitant little yes was going to change my life forever.

❑❑

Chapter Six

Working at the Grassroots

My work with SEWA was supposed to be time-bound so I continued my UPSC exam preparation too. My current work and my career goals were different, I thought.

I had begun my stint with SEWA working with women fruit and vegetable vendors in Jehangirpuri, which was a good thirty kilometers away from JNU. My routine now comprised daily trips to and fro, as I hit the ground to better understand the issues faced by these women. They suffered daily harassment at the hands of police and municipal authorities, and the absence of a proper licensing system for selling adding to their woes. In addition, they did not have any bank accounts, so saving to further their small businesses was out of question. The insensitivity of local police was such that rather than lending a helping hand, they actually looked to extract money from these impoverished women.

I continued meeting these women for weeks, conversing with them at their place of work, understanding their living conditions and trying to picture their day to day lives in as much detail as possible. As their stories began getting more vivid, I couldn't stop my heart from opening up completely. Listening to them was taxing; I heard so many stories of difficulties, abuse, and complexities. The infectious spirit of optimism that carried all of them through life only added to the wretchedness of my experience. How easily we take our privileges for granted. How easily do we complain. How simply do we ignore the squalor and marginalization which co-exists with our bubbles of fine living.

I was developing a unique bond with these women, built on daily mutual exchange and conversations. These women were tough – perseverance and mental strength characterized them. Theirs was a different kind of life, and I had been able to win their trust enough to become privy to the minutest details. While a part of me felt burdened with their narratives, the other raged to do something, to stand for them and effect a change. They, strangers till so recently, now occupied my thoughts, and conversations with them went on in my head long after they had left.

The purpose of all our talking was not limited to helping them unburden or giving them someone to trust; it was also to strategize and arrive at common solutions to their daily troubles.

We made decisions on how to organize women into Self-Help Groups. These were collective units of ten to twenty women, initiated into saving a small amount of money every month to create a fund, from which they could borrow internally as needed. The process seemed simple enough, but our first roadblock was their illiteracy: most of them could not even sign their names.

We had to begin at actual ground zero, so I started teaching them. We practiced their signatures, and the women showed such enthusiasm and had so much fun learning that I was elated.

The next step was to approach banks to open SHG accounts. I saw in person how apathetic the bankers were to understanding the background and needs of these women. They were categorically dismissive. Although the RBI (Reserve Bank of India) had passed an official notification mandating the opening of SHG (Self Help Group) accounts in all banks, the banks often hid within self-fashioned procedural complications of dubious legality to deny our request. This, despite our providing all the necessary documentation and following due process. The lack of basic human courtesy accorded these women broke my heart. No one inquired after the reason for their visit. No one asked them to sit. The visit of these women elicited insulting wonder and disdain. Bank officials wanted only to talk to me; conversing with these women was beneath their dignity. The women themselves had internalized this sense of inferiority. They were comfortable being ignored. Had been conditioned thus. The attitude of bankers wasn't any different from the attitude of life in general towards them.

"Sanjay bhai, don't disturb yourself over us. This is normal," they told me. "This is our fate. This is the fate of all the poor in our country. That you are helping us is enough." Somehow these words, while definitely touching, never managed to console me. My feeling of wretchedness at the status quo continued. And I always pulled in the women leaders into conversations with the officials. They wouldn't be left invisible if I could help it.

After meeting four banks over a period of two months with all our homework in place, and being turned down, my patience had reached its limit. I was frustrated; the women were not! And for them, I had to stay positive. I had to keep working.

Finally, someone directed us to the Azadpur Mandi branch of the Bank of Baroda. This was going to be our final destination in the quest for the SHG accounts. The Branch Manager Mr. Arun Tiwari was very warm, and receptive of our request. He had heard about work done by SEWA and by its founder Ela-ben Bhatt. He readily agreed to open three SHG accounts in his bank, with a promise to facilitate the way for more in future. Going one human step further, he also treated these women with respect. They were seated and offered tea. One small courtesy extended in acknowledgment of people for who they were – humans, deserving dignity and respect.

* * *

I met Mr. Tiwari at a Roundtable on Financial Inclusion a few years ago; he had become CMD of Union Bank of India. I reminded him the help he extended sixteen years ago, and he seemed pleased to be reminded; despite his seniority there were no airs whatsoever. His manner of remaining true to his job and helping those who needed and deserved it, I am sure (and hope), has done much to ensure he reaches the pinnacle of his profession.

* * *

When you witness someone else's struggles at such close quarters, it turns you more sensitive than simply facing your own problems. When I started interacting with municipal authorities and policemen to figure out how these vendors could effectively earn their living, without facing undue obstacles or having their dignity stripped, I felt raw.

These women travelled twenty kilometers to Chandini Chowk each day. When livelihood beckoned, after all, one went any distance, but to what avail? After such hard work and effort, they had to both pay daily bribes and conduct their affairs in fear. Municipal authorities would never regulate this segment; it would lose them their bribes. Chaos favored the corrupt. And for the women, any prospect of saving was washed away. While I was living through this ordeal, I resolved to do my bit for changing the way authorities interacted with hapless citizens, and hence opted for IPS as my preference in the Civil Services exam.

I became increasingly aware of the distinction between theory and practice. University was all about intellectual debates, but there was little or no focus on bringing about actual change. The world outside did not care for theory, because when push came to shove, one had to argue promptly against short-sightedness. Discussions on campus were good to participate in, but not always realistic. They were locked within the romance of theory, which dealt too often only on abstractions. Reality was gruesome and needed doers to take over from the thinkers.

* * *

I could not get through Mains, though I scored well and my marks were good enough to proceed to the interview stage in next attempt. Logic dictated that I get back to my studies and prepare for attempting the civil services exam a second time following my seven months with SEWA. The decision, however, was no longer simple.

I wanted a secure career, social security for my family, and the chance to lead a comfortable life. All this would come to pass as an IAS or an IPS officer. They were illustrious career streams, and I could go on doing good work and effecting real, on-the-ground changes. I had however gotten attached to the work I did with the vendors. I knew SEWA couldn't offer me anything in terms of money and material compensation; their Delhi wing was new and as yet did not have a stable funding. But this did not bother me as much as the issues the women faced - they had become my own, and fighting for them seemed the most natural course. I had myself internalized the troubles they faced. Leaving them midway seemed out of question. The situation seemed a classic heart versus mind dilemma. What to pay heed to?

* * *

The women I met at Jehangirpuri were very kind and loving. I used to sit with them for hours and listen to their stories. I also spent time with their children – young and grown-up – and understand their psycho-emotional and economic problems. The entire community exuded natural affection and it felt like we all had a tangible cord of deep connection running through us.

I couldn't offer a solution to each of their problems, but I could listen with empathy. And that I did. Perhaps I was a refreshing connection to the outer world, one which had thus far only been cruel on them. And in their presence I felt valued. For each of them, from the youngest to the oldest, I was 'Sanjay bhai'. It was as if 'bhai' - brother - had become my surname.

I think what helped me get so comfortable so quickly, with them was that I came from a small town and had seen financial struggle closely. They offered me a chair or requested I sit on their beds, but I felt at ease sitting on the floor with them. Even this simple act of choosing to sit on the floor became symbolic of dissolving artificial boundaries between us.

My seven-months with SEWA had had clearly defined engagement and output areas but what I ended up doing was far beyond the scope of my work. A certain magic was put in motion – things were happening on their own. We were driving each other.

On the other hand my disenchantment with JNU and academia kept growing, this time for a new reason. Fellow students who had qualified for the Civil Services started behaving like demigods. Their crude natures out in the open, they suddenly seemed to feel they descended from another planet. It wasn't the rule, but it happened enough for me to sense a pattern. Even when they came to visit the campus on a break from training, they were disconnected, their earlier life and community seemed no longer worth associating with. In a few cases the arrogance of being an Officer of the Government was very obvious. Witnessing this was demotivating, and I often wondered whether this was who I aspired to be, really.

These people who had now sipped the first taste of success felt they were now the 'class' and everyone else was the 'mass'. Most came from humble, middle-class backgrounds, and it seemed dealing with overnight success defeated them. These officers wanted to behave a certain way and project a certain image, forgetting the primary purposes of their offices or the vision with which they had set out to serve civil life.

* * *

It was time to make my decision. My tenure with SEWA was ending and I was seriously rethinking my civil services ambition. I was sure I wanted to help bring about a real change in the lives of those afflicted by poverty, but what course of action and which medium to choose? I could bring about 'greater' change as an officer of the government, with the public machinery to support my effort. But I doubted more and more whether I would remain the same Sanjaybhai if I rose or wished to rise in the ranks, and began to believe I too would succumb to the quicksand of success and start treating myself and others differently. Would power and comfort trap me in an elite bubble, or would I be able to remain 'common' and thus work for issues as though they were my own? Haunted by these questions I sat down for a discussion with Renana-ben, the chairperson of SEWA Bharat, on my future.

She was pleased with my young resolve to build a career with SEWA, but reminded me of the alternative, and asked me whether

I was prepared to leave the power, prestige, and comfort that came with being a civil servant in India. Was I prepared to give all that up, along with respect and stability afforded by the career? Her questions were pertinent, but speaking with her only clarified that all this had lost meaning for me. I *was* clear about where I wanted to engage my energies. She happily agreed to renew my contract. The women of Jehangirpuri too were extremely happy to hear of this turn of affairs.

This was among the most sensible decisions in my life. The short engagement of seven months was going to transform into a passionate involvement lasting seventeen years.

* * *

I was convinced of the import of the work I was going to do. I felt joyous. My father had retired and my elder brother was supporting me financially; I ought to give back to the family. But I set these worries aside, kept my head and heart balanced with the conviction that even with the very humble start at SEWA I could manage to survive well and enjoy a decent life.

I did not appear for the civil services exam next year. The goal of my life had not changed, but the path I had chosen to take had. My aim was to serve the invisible in this country, but I was not going to be rich in resources and support of administrative machinery. To compensate, I had the strength of the people I would serve. SEWA was now my path, my means to the goal of national service through empowering women.

I had grown up in a place where goddesses were worshipped, but actual women were desecrated and oppressed. Society and its practices were stacked against women. Instances of wife-beating were common. Husbands did not think twice before abandoning their wives if dowry was insufficient. One heard constantly of gruesome deaths caused by the greed of in-laws. In homes like ours boys and girls were treated differently, their gendered roles defined rigidly. Movement and access for girls was severely restricted. I had been pained to see such practices since early childhood. And how with greater exposure, after learning about the debilitating problems women faced because of them, I knew more clearly how wrong they were, and that they needed to be completely weeded out for our society to have any hope of prospering. You cannot recognize and worship the power of Durga while pushing the women in your own house into subservience.

Someone very close to my own family faced much humiliation for not being able to fulfil the dowry expectations. She had undergone her own share of torture, which I had been witness to in my formative years. All this was stored in my memory as a deep gash.

Women are regarded as objects of pleasure. Their existence is reduced to a body which exists for the purpose of pleasuring the male. Within domestic environs, a woman's responsibility is producing and nurturing progeny. Her movement is limited and autonomy and agency denied. If economic circumstances force her to work, she is regarded as a secondary bread-winner even if she works longer and harder than the male. Seldom is she granted the choice to be financially independent. The boundaries on her movement and agency too are agnostic of socio-economic background, with exploitation being visible at all levels.

In sharp contradiction to the man, a woman is expected to take care of the domestic chores even if she is working for long hours. To make matters worse, she almost always earns lesser than the male counterpart. During my stint with SEWA, I once had a long argument with a garment factory owner about giving fair wages to the artisans of SEWA Delhi. His response was shocking, "Why do you bother for their wages, Sir? It is only pocket money for them."

The mindset is sickening and it needs to undergo a drastic change. This garment factory owner reduced the legitimate economic contribution a woman makes to her family as 'pocket money'. He also failed to recognize the women as equal and independent members of the society, his male existence entitling him to belittle the women. This stereotyping of women is not restricted to any particular domain, one can see it sports, journalism, science and technology, and every other professional field. In both government and the private sector, women's presence in the top echelons is rare. Women in high positions remains a big city phenomenon, still not cascading down to tier 2 and 3 cities and villages. Women are mostly given leg work in the informal economy which comprises over 90 percent of the total work force in India. Women are the laborers, whereas all the supervisors are male.

Equality of the sexes is a far cry in our country. Understanding and accepting women as equal human beings, as well as recognizing their contributions in all spheres, is a starting point to bring about a change. I do believe it is women who lend stability to the society and to our personal lives. We should acknowledge them as a powerful half in our world and do our bit to build a more equitable society, where women are encouraged to enjoy their full potential. They need to be able to step out of the confinement of their homes and be visible on the streets, markets, offices and workplaces – everywhere in the country, in equal numbers and dignity.

* * *

Society, community, and even workplaces might be against them, but the women I was working with or for were inherently very strong. My work with SEWA was also a lesson in recognizing their strength and spirit.

My work involved decision-making through negotiations with government officials, political leaders, donor organizations, partners, etc. Conflict and dilemma where so many stakeholders are involved is only normal. The guiding mantra became, "How will this impact the women of SEWA? Will it benefit them only in the short run? Are they likely to benefit from this decision in the long run?" As soon as I found answers to all these questions, taking decisions was easy.

I was always reminded too of Gandhiji's words – "I will give you a talisman. Whenever you are in doubt, or when the self becomes too much with you, apply the following test. Recall the face of the poorest and the weakest man [woman] whom you may have seen, and ask yourself, if the step you contemplate is going to be of any use to him [her]. Will he [she] gain anything by it? Will it restore him [her] to a control over his [her] own life and destiny?

In other words, will it lead to swaraj [freedom] for the hungry and spiritually starving millions? Then you will find your doubts and yourself melt away."

Working with the underprivileged and marginalized was every moment rewarding. Some moments were like priceless jewels, when you knew you had accomplished something in the interest of gender parity, generally or in a specific way, or when you had cracked a negotiation likely to change someone's life forever and for good.

Santosh-ben, a 22-year old, young, married woman became an entrepreneur after quitting her job with SEWA. She had to quit to look after her child, but I strongly advised her to not discontinue work. She had undergone training as a beautician, and I suggested she start her own beauty parlor and an associated training center. When I met her a year later I found her institute has about 120 regular students and was thriving! She had also started tailoring classes for young girls, and her face radiated the joy of independence and accomplishment. She was driving her own fate and that of many young women in her community. From an employee at SEWA, she had become an entrepreneur with her own staff and students. Many girls like Santosh graduated from SEWA's skill development classes and went on to do things not just for themselves, but for other women too. Empowering one woman does empower a whole community.

I feel tremendous joy remembering these powerful women, so inspiring for the way they took their destiny into their own hands and crafted their own futures.

* * *

My interaction with Leela-ben, one of the leaders of SEWA Delhi, taught me a lot. She is a powerful example of an empowered woman with a robust understanding of the entire spectrum of issues related to women. An approachable leader, she was my personal sounding board whenever I needed advice. She had spent considerable time going around the city, exchanging clothes for utensils – a trader in her own right. Her door-to-door interactions with customers, police, and municipal authorities had made her street-smart and wise. She knew her way around difficulties and could innovate and think on her feet. Her work had also exposed her to issues in all their nakedness, her vessel of understanding brimming with the diversity of problems harrowing women everywhere.

It was Leela-ben who educated me most about sexual harassment in informal workplaces. She discussed her daughters' harassment in markets, and my eyes started opening up to this abhorrent truth as they never had before. Later, I learned to see how rampant the abuse and suppression of women is all around us is – caste, background, social strata no bar – and was driven to writing articles in national dailies about them.

Leela ben always challenged me, pushing me to do better for the sake of the street vendors. I loved the trust she posed in me, and each day spent observing her was a lesson – how she understood issues, how she dealt with people, how she prioritized. She was fierce and fearless.

Once, she went to the Republic of Benin to attend a global conference. The organizers had bought an airplane ticket only for her, with no accompaniment. Everyone in the office was worried, since Leela-ben had never travelled alone on an airplane before. But knowing Leela-ben, I was confident she would not only manage to travel well, but would have a significant impact on people she met at the conference. I asked my colleagues to write down the flight details in Hindi and Gujarati, and we organized a mock drill. Although she was upset with the organizers for not facilitating a ticket for someone to accompany her, she was comfortable with the idea of travelling alone. As I expected, not only did she travel successfully, also efficiently used her platform to back the cause of street vendors and share their actual conditions and problems.

We were overjoyed and welcomed her back with a ceremony in which, other than the experiences in Benin, she shared how it felt to journey alone. I can hear her now: "I was thrilled when I got to know that I would be travelling to a foreign country. Do you know, in my family, I am the first person to travel abroad? This thrill lasted till I was told I have to travel alone. I was so upset. At one point I thought I will just say no to Sanjay bhai and tell him

I cannot go on this journey all by myself… I am fortunate that I have colleagues like you who supported me and explained every part of the journey in great detail. I am glad I could undertake this trip and share the agony of Delhi's women street vendors on an international platform. The experience also opened my eyes to the plight of women in many other countries, who are suffering in similar ways. I am carrying back loads of knowledge and a renewed self-confidence, and I am happy to be back amongst all of you..." That was how she always spoke - of herself as part of a whole.

* * *

SEWA stood for the collective strength and the collectivization of women. When women came together on one platform and raised their voices for a cause, the experience was powerful and transformative.

Another time, in the year 2000, I was to organize a leadership training for the women from Jehangirpuri in Ahmedabad. Excited with the idea, I shared it with Kari-ben and other leaders. Their faces, instead of reciprocating my excitement, became tense. They said their husbands would not let them go. Stumped for a moment, but responsible for further skilling these women and sending them to Ahmedabad, I could only invite them not to miss this opportunity to increase their collective strength and lead their own movements.

They understood, but their problem was very real too. They promised to talk to their husbands and get back to us, but solving this problem was not going to be simple. A few days later, whispers reached their community and caste leaders. They threatened the women with ostracism and what amounted to excommunicating families if husbands 'allowed' their wives to travel without a male companion. The threat imminent and real, the women met with me again.

The situation was difficult, but now was not the time to give up. "Don't give in," I told them. "If you give in now, you will have surrendered control over your lives once again, to these leaders and husbands. Take a stand. Go to Ahmedabad. Taking this stand is your first lesson in leadership skills."

Much discussion and deliberation later, they said in one voice– We will go to Ahmedabad, come what may!

Once they had conquered the fears and subservience in their own hearts, the battle became a lot easier. A meeting was called by the community leaders, where they asked for the women to provide a 'physical guarantee' that they would return safely without indulging in any act that could bring ill-repute to their family name and community honor. Absurd as it may be, these regressive notions control patriarchal brains still. A man does all he can to restrict the movement and independence of 'his' woman, lest she be 'polluted' by coming in touch with other men. By a 'physical guarantee', they meant that the group of women needed to find a man who could stand up in their support and who would be held responsible if any untoward incident happened. Unequivocally regressive though it was, the condition needed to be met if our women were to travel to Ahmedabad. A few tense moments later they were able to find support in the form of a young, progressive lad from the community, who agreed to be their guarantee.

There was a new determination in their eyes; I knew they were unstoppable now. All of them travelled to Ahmedabad together - their first independent trip out - unchaperoned by any male family member. The boundary had been breached. After this, the husbands and local leaders never stopped them.

* * *

Education was a major concern in this group. Some of the women were very keen to get their children the best education possible. It was not a frivolous dream, but a very real ambition. They understood the import of education in turning the lives of people around and opening the world of opportunities up for their children. They were driven almost to desperation in their attempt to generate funds for education, but even this desperation was inspirational, for it reflected a call to change and improve their lived conditions.

Basanti-ben was a young widow with a son. Being of a constitutionally Scheduled Caste, she had to face the worst of society when she was widowed; she as homeless as well. She lived at the Community Centre with her mother and single child.

When Basanti-ben became a part of a SEWA Bharat project that focused on collecting waste from residential areas, the first thing she did with the money was to send her son to a private English-medium school. She called me up to share this big news. "Sanjay bhai, I am the proudest mother today! My son is now admitted to a private English-medium school and I wanted to share this moment of joy with you." I was touched beyond words. I congratulated her. The joy was hers, but she had made my day. At a later occasion, during a meeting with the Deputy CM of Bihar–Sushil Modi, she brought her son to Patna and proudly introduced him around.

* * *

Sangita-ben from Munger was another visionary woman. She had been unable to support her son's and daughter's education on their meager family income. Her husband reared cattle and farmed, while she worked as an incense-stick roller. Her dedication to work was truly exceptional and she soon caught my attention. During my interaction with her, I learned that it was, again, the desire to send her kids to school that drove her to work so hard. Seeing continuous diligence and dedication, I got her inducted as Supervisor for one of our centers. She understood the work of rolling incense sticks, after all, and the quality expected. The change in role brought better payment, which she promptly directed towards her children's study. Her son dreamt of studying Computer Engineering and she made sure she supported him in realizing that dream as well as she possibly could. Recently, she joyfully informed me that her son Navnit graduated as a Computer Engineer from a government college in Bihar.

* * *

Many young female colleagues of mine had poor educational credentials, but they more than compensated through hard work, talent, and lot of undiscovered potential. They were the stars of our organization. Due to their association with SEWA, many were able to rejoin school or college and proceeded with more confidence. These were our upwardly mobile stalwarts, inspiring other girls through their journeys.

I was on a constant quest to unearth potential latent within these women and help them find bigger roles within the organization. Talent and hard work should never go unnoticed and unrewarded. One such woman started as a teacher and went on to become the manager of the credit cooperative and then the CEO of a social enterprise. Another who started as a teacher eventually became a Union Leader. Many others rose up to the level of coordinators. During their association with SEWA, many married and had babies. As an organization, we were very sensitive to the changes going on in the personal lives of our female colleagues. We would be accommodative and try and help in the effort to look after their kids. On many occasions, even if we were hurting on a professional front, I had to be silent in the interest of respecting personal compulsions. These women were the support systems of the organization, having built it with us brick by brick; the least we could do was reciprocate.

* * *

When my own son Chaitanya was a few months old, we moved into our new house situated in Vasundhara Enclave which was close to my wife's office. She worked with the TV news channel Sahara Samay. Her company was decidedly not accommodative; her workplace was plain insensitive to motherhood and the conditions which accompany it. She was given night-shifts, discounting the need to be with her very small baby. Although I was taking care of Chaitanya, Seema was still feeding him. This was long before breast pumps became the norm that puts nursing mothers back to work faster - so, I had to drive down to her office each night and she would come out to feed him. It was an unpleasant routine, but we were helpless. Seema's commitment could have been eased through a superior's intervention, but she was not one of her bosses' 'favorites'. Quitting the job was also not an option, since we had recently bought a house and had to repay the loans.

Such a harrowing personal experience further cemented my belief in looking after and supporting women, especially when their personal circumstances became demanding. It was also not merely a matter of obligation. Supporting women and being a wholesome part of their lives also gave me great joy. From dealing with grassroots challenges to negotiating government authorities and engaging at the policy level, every bit was an immense learning experience.

Women members, leaders, and colleagues at SEWA were family to me, and would always remain thus. We built bonds over 17 years, through which I learned lessons of courage, happiness, optimism, and contentment. Such lessons couldn't be encapsulated in a text or taught in a classroom any more than my JNU professor's experiences as Foreign Secretary could. Their drive to do better for themselves was a challenge to me too, to enhance my skills and abilities. Such experiences nourish the essence – the atma– of a person and teach them what it truly means to be human in this world. ❑❑

Chapter Seven

Dream Home

The monsoon of 1987 was terrible.

Katihar is a flood prone area. Water logging was common in our low-lying areas, where our house too was located. During the monsoon it rained incessantly for days and the sound of thunderstorms would force us all into a huddle. It was scary, for the family but especially for us children, who were young; our only solace was the gentle presence of Maa and Babuji watching over us.

In 1987 rains wrecked their usual havoc, this time with a fiercer fury. The accompanying thunderstorms and lightning added to the chaos. We were scared, for water had started seeping into our house rapidly and the rains showed no signs of abating. At this point, we were living in the semi pucca house my father had worked so hard building. His hard work, alas, was going to be washed away in just a few hours. It wasn't a fancy construction; it was, simply, home.

In no time, our house was half-drowned. We could all see it coming apart. Our meager belongings were already submerged. Worry crumpled my Maa and Babuji's faces but they were quick to act and ensure the safety and security of their family. The situation was so grave we had to build boats out of the stem of Banana plants to keep ourselves afloat. Drenched and worried, we managed to reach my uncle's home somehow, and stayed there till the water around our home sank away.

It was after this devastating flood and series of thunderstorms which completely destroyed our house that my father decided to undertake a cement and brick construction instead.

* * *

In my childhood I had lived in huts, then in a semi-pucca and finally in a pucca construction. I have fond memories of the time spent close together as a family and of our community, but it does not negate the very real difficulties we lived through, where basic shelter was concerned. We lived with little and even so instability or the threat of instability loomed large. Our home couldn't withstand the chicaneries of weather.

Growing up, the need for a stable shelter became important. I had to have a house of my own which afforded my family the comfort and safety that I couldn't have as a child.

My own family unit had become a reality by this point. I had found a wonderful partner in Seema, who understood my concerns, motivations, and mindset. She and I had a chance meeting during an Abida Parveen concert. Though I had little inkling at that time that we would eventually tie the knot, we hit it off wonderfully well in the first go. The one thing about Seema which greatly charmed me was that despite having been born and brought up in Delhi, her roots lay in Bihar. She loved everything about Bihar – the culture, colours, culinary traditions, and artforms. After the concert we kept in touch and soon, started seeing each other. Within a few months we solicited the blessings of our parents who happily agreed to our marriage.

Seema is a bold and confident woman, who didn't shy away from raising her voice against any injustice. Her views on society's gender divide were firm and loud, and she advocated parity in all spheres. Her father was a migrant from Bihar who had worked hard to bring up his children in the capital city. Seema embodied the same spirit of hard work and spent her early years excelling in journalism, despite not having a formal degree in it. Her heart, however, remains in the arts. This passion for them blossomed and unfurled further as the years passed on.

* * *

Life with Seema was moving along just fine. It was in late 2003 that I made up my mind - we had to own a house before we had a child. "You do know you have no deposit and you cannot go to your father for financial help?" asked Seema, upon hearing my plans. How was I suddenly driven by this manic idea? I wanted both, desperately – a child and a house. And I wanted a house now, to ensure our baby had a stable, wholesome existence. Living in rented apartments and shifting time and again wasn't my idea of stability or wholesomeness.

I was of course involved in the social sector. My wife was working in media. We weren't sure whether we could manage the payments even together, but I knew we had to try. To make matters more complex, my wife had in a condition: the house had to be in Delhi, not in Noida or Ghaziabad. She believed Delhi was safer, and I wouldn't have known how to argue. Thus the grand hunt for an ideal house began.

Considering property rates and proximity to my wife's office, we decided to search for a flat in East Delhi. I zeroed in on Vasundhara Enclave. A couple of other good areas, Mayur Vihar and Patparganj, were way beyond our budget. Truth be told we didn't have a budget. In the absence of any savings, we were dependent on the liberalization of the home loan market. I started visiting property dealers every alternate day to find a decent apartment within a reasonable price bracket. A month later, we still had not reached anywhere.

Then suddenly, we both fell ill, simultaneously. The diagnosis for both of us was the same – jaundice. In addition, Seema was by now already pregnant. The situation became stressful, and we had a lot to deal with. The house hunt had to be called off for three months – the period of complete bed-rest prescribed for us by the doctor. Fortunately, Seema's pregnancy was normal; at least one thing was going right, and it was a source of endless optimism and excitement for us.

* * *

A three-month long convalescence later, I was back in the office of the property dealer. The first news to greet me – property prices had gone up in the past three months. Well, not a great start.

The dealer took us around. I wanted a three BHK (bedrooms, hallway, kitchen) bearing in mind our future needs and healthy living. He took me to an apartment I had seen three months ago, but this time there as a 5 percent hike in price.

I couldn't do much about the increase in price. The apartment was nice, well-ventilated, spacious, with a lot of natural light streaming in. Since it had not been put to use after its completion, the interiors were dirty and dingy, but that could be fixed. The good location was a bonus. After checking most of our mental boxes, we decided to go ahead with the purchase.

A meeting was fixed with the owner at the dealer's office. We were to carry some cash and a cheque book. At the end of the meeting, the dealer asked us to give Rs 50,000 in cash and a post-dated cheque of 1.5 lakh rupees to the owner. My wife and I stared at each other, in shock and embarrassment. We did not have that much cash. We were only carrying 25,000 rupees between us. It was the beginning of the month and even with both our salaries, we had barely 28,000 rupees in our account. The entire month's expenses had to be accounted for and worry must have veiled our faces.

The property dealer was a perceptive man and he guessed something was amiss. We were honest about our situation – what else could we do? There was no problem with handing over a post-dated cheque; the payment could be managed within a week with the help of family and friends. The cash posed a challenge. The property dealer took 25,000 from his table drawer and handed to the owner on our behalf. He told us we could return the amount later. At that time he seemed like a little divine intervener to help us seal the deal.

The agreement to sell was made, and we were given 40 days to make the final payment and get the house transferred in our name.

The real challenge now stared us in the face – how were we to manage the loan?

* * *

We started contacting bank agents to figure out which bank could loan us the maximum amount. There is an undeniable absurdity to our decision: we had no money, truly. But this very approach has often accomplished great goals. We decided to act, and solved the million problems which came along, along the way.

It was brought to our notice that ICICI Bank was the most accommodative of atypical home loan requests at the time. We got all our documentation in order and applied to ICICI for a joint loan. The joint loan was necessary since our individual incomes were too low to qualify. It took us about ten days to decide on the bank, and we now had thirty days to pay the balance.

After ten days of processing, I was informed that the bank had declined my request for a loan, while my wife's application had been approved. The reason was simple – my wife was working with a private sector media house, while I worked in an NGO.

I was crestfallen. Here I was, working for the cause of bettering the lived conditions of the poor and all this work was an obstacle to achieving my own dreams. Something had to be done lest I lose this opportunity.

* * *

The Executive Director of ICICI Bank at that point was Mr. Nachiket More. He had once come to attend a workshop on pensions organized by SEWA Bank. I met him briefly there, and had his card. The day my application was declined his name came to my mind and I thought of reaching out.

I had his email address and decided to write to him. In his speech at the workshop, More had mentioned that his bank was keen on reaching out to poor women with micro-finance opportunities. In my email, I asked him, if his bank did not trust someone who worked for the women associated with SEWA, what chance did they really have with the micro-financing prospects? My email was genuine, polite, but I minced no words to put my opinion across.

In exactly two days I received an email from the Delhi Regional Head, stating that my case had been referred by the Executive Director, and would be addressed on priority. I was overjoyed. Things had been set in motion. The bank approached me with a request for some further information and miscellaneous documents, but I was definitely going to be granted the loan now.

The final day of the payment was approaching. The bank said that I could get 80 percent of the total value of the apartment price, but my financial condition required at least 90 percent of the total value. In addition, some funds were needed for furniture and fixtures. I wrote to the Regional Manager, citing my condition. The bank, again, was very responsive and my request was approved and processed shortly thereafter.

Within the next few days, on the 13th August 2004, just 19 days to Chaitanya's birth, the apartment was ours!

* * *

I still get goosebumps thinking of the whole episode. A decision made at a whim, if backed by strong reasoning, could prove fruitful, through just keeping going. I had to have a house before I expanded my family. It sounded crazy even to Seema at the start; she laughed it off. Her laughter was valid, given the poor state of our finances – we simply didn't have any!

Still, she supported my decision, and was valiant through our adventure. We knew our goal, but had no idea which path to take, so we strode forth in the direction immediately before us.

Seema has been a partner in the true sense of the word. At the same time, she has been firmly moving ahead in her own professional trajectory. Her last years in journalism didn't work out too well, and the fighter in her refused to give in. When she was absolutely sure that as a woman who wouldn't compromise on her terms, media couldn't afford her a career, she decided to quit and start her own short-film production company, which has since been running successfully.

In addition, she also developed an enterprise called 'Roots Tale', which is steepened in the folk Madhubani art form of Bihar.

Seema herself learnt the art form and thoroughly immersed herself into connecting traditions with the demands of the market. And in this mission, she has done well. Witnessing her growth as an artist and entrepreneur, simultaneously, has been a source of joy and pride for me.

Seema is a fiercely independent woman, and I value her independence. This doesn't mean we do not have our share of fights and arguments. We do, but it is a shared respect and love which helps us find a way, always.

When I look back at the entire episode I am struck by two realizations. One, I have been eminently fortunate. A slew of events, circumstances, people and their actions, needed to come together in a perfect moment, for me to realize this dream for my little family. The property dealer who paid for us, my friend Ajay who kept me going through the search for a home through his own as a struggling lawyer was no less difficult, accompanying me on visits and jollying me along and Nachiket More, who helped me getting the loan from ICICI Bank. And these are only individual instances. Because of them my family still live in the same home, where Chaitanya grew up and where Tathya is growing apace.

And my gratitude has made me reconsider other events, other junctures, and acknowledge that my development has been steered to success in a way that is uncommon. Nevertheless I maintain that old adage: success is perseverance, through uncertainty, sometimes with blind faith but mostly with careful consideration for all possible contingencies and consequences, perseverance even when one's ambitions look like they are being derailed. A path appears - sometimes not one you anticipated, sometimes one that takes a good deal of openness to even recognise as a possible path - and if your essential goal is clear to you, you can make your way to it regardless of derailments and accidents.

And finally, there is no separating one's professional attitudes from one's personal. They say the personal is political. It is professional too. Perseverance is a habit - and it is the habit of commitment to one's private life that makes one able to commit to the public.

❑❑

Chapter Eight

The Creative Challenge

I had my first proper trial with a camera in 1989, when I was sixteen. I went to the nearby village of Mansahi with Ramesh bhaiya. The village had a beautiful, idyllic railway bridge with greenery all around. It made for the perfect shoot location. With this landscape in the background, we became the subjects for each other and clicked away!

When the pictures came out, Ramesh bhaiya, complimented me on my photography skills and advised that I continue with photography. But how could I? We were shooting with an SLR camera and these cameras were expensive. Also, since I was not doing well in studies, pursuing an interest like photography was completely out of the question.

Growing up in Katihar posed many challenges, which continued well into later life. When you live off limited means, having a passion or hobby does not really mean anything. This doesn't mean you don't dream, obviously. Dreams and interests are involuntary; they creep into your subconscious, and often stay locked there, in a latent subterranean region of your brain, getting buried deeper and deeper under stress of pragmatic, pressing concerns.

The sojourn with Ramesh bhaiya had created in me a secret desire – to look at the world through the lens of a camera and capture frames to freeze, forever. This, of course, remained unspoken till adulthood. When I became aware of this desire, cameras were family assets. They were luxury goods. I couldn't 'own' one, being too young, and I could never ask my family, our means were too modest.

I began by borrowing cameras from my friends – the ones which needed a photo roll out of which pictures were developed in a studio. In our time, Japanese cameras had entered the Indian market and sales were fast picking up. Many acquaintances from Katihar bought these Japanese cameras from Biratngar.

Biratnagar was *the* hub for Japanese and Chinese electronic items and clothes. Since we did not possess a camera, our family used to borrow them for special occasions. Later, my eldest brother, Arun bhaiya had bought a new Minolta SLR for his work, which I borrowed a few times to learn how to use it and figure out how it worked. I also asked the owner of Shadow Studio to teach me basic photography skills, and he was kind enough to oblige.

I saw the transition from black and white to color photography - photography was to me, and has remained even through digital photography, magic. There was a tradition of preserving a family photo album when we were growing up. With the advent of digicams and smartphones that practice has bitten the dust. What has vanished along with these photo albums are the fond moments one spent pouring over the photos again and again, and reliving special days and times. I loved doing this. I loved revisiting special figments of my memories, guided by these pictures. Photography allowed one to freeze time itself – how amazing, isn't it? Equally amazing, that it took me two decades for this desire to find expression.

* * *

My desire resurfaced when I began work with SEWA, in fact. There were so many scenes I wanted to capture and freeze in time – women deeply engrossed in a task, performing intricate tasks with precision and concentration, multitasking between home and work, taking care of their children while meticulously fulfilling responsibilities. From the perspiration on their foreheads to the smile of accomplishment on their faces – I wanted to capture it all and share their stories with the world.

I had begun visiting the India Habitat Centre quite frequently for work. Each time, I witnessed some or other photography exhibition in multiple locations at the venue. Stopping to stare into these pictures further heightened my yearning to pursue photography again.

In one such IHC meeting I was accompanied by Renana-ben, and as we strolled about looking at photographs, I said I too would like to click pictures like those. She asked, "Do you also want to put on an exhibition like this?" Did I? I wasn't sure, so I just shrugged. That was the end of our brief conversation, but it was the seed of an idea.

Renana-ben's question was reframed in my mind. "Are you committed enough to pull off an exhibition like this?" I did have the passion but was a decided amateur. So I laid the idea to rest. For a while longer.

One of our program managers from a partner organization in the UK called to say they had a small budget for us to spend on communications. If we had something in mind, they could support it. We certainly had something in mind – a creative communication project that could showcase the stories of our women warriors. This was our chance - and mine, to unearth the buried idea about photography and utilize it for a cause I was involved in. Why not invest in a good SLR camera, click in-action pictures of our women members and develop postcards, calendars or stand-alone photographs to be used as SEWA communication material? It would work.

* * *

I had no idea what the budget was, but I did discuss a conservative figure with Bethan, the Asia Program Manager at One World Action, UK, to put the initial resources and projections in place. She and I were later delighted to realize we would perhaps have more funding than my projection. She kept pushing me to think harder, if more funding was available, what would I do to highlight the plight and the successes of the women engaged in the informal sector? My thoughts needed expansion, and within a week, I came up with a concept note to document the lives and stories of our women in the form of pictures, which would be showcased as a travelling exhibition, and be compiled in a photo-book. From cards and calendars, we had evolved to exhibitions and books!

I was skeptical about the kind of response we would get from the partner organization, though. The idea had gotten bigger, and so had the budget - significantly so. Thankfully, they appreciated the idea, and were keen to support our efforts to develop strong outward communication for SEWA. They now wanted an understanding of the finer details.

We had a conference call, where the Head of International Partnerships, Andy Rutherford, was on line. He asked, "Sanjay, this is a fantastic idea, but who is going to execute it?" My immediate response was, "Me!"

This response, too eager, was in retrospect perhaps amateurish. Andy did not sound convinced. "Are you a photographer?," he inquired. I said I wasn't a professional but could compose good photos... Coincidentally, I was traveling to London for a conference soon, and Andy requested I click some pictures and carry them along. "Sure," I said.

I had to prove my skill, practically. I donned the student hat again, and asked a friend Manish from Katihar for some quick tips. Then I went to Sunder Nagri, one of the communities where I was engaged. In this little, nondescript urban locality near Dilshad Garden in Delhi, weavers, shoemakers, and bangle makers operated out of ramshackle shops and workshops. Here is where I spent my first hours as a photographer, catching hard work, skill, commitment, emotion, and dismal living conditions within the frame of my camera, all against the backdrop of incessant chaos and clamor. The assignment was a tiring, taxing but satisfying. What we received as final prints were pictures which spoke louder than any elaborate text cold. These frames were a hit with our UK partners, and I heaved a sigh of relief.

In London Andy lauded my work but also expressed another concern: "Will you be able to devote time to this photography project given your other roles and responsibilities?" This was a legitimate concern, and came with advice to consider hiring a professional to deliver on the project.

Pondering his question and the advice for a while, I responded, "But I don't think a professional can deliver with as much passion as someone involved in this work personally... This concept is unique and heartfelt, and I am confident that I am the best person to do both – click the pictures and author the book... I really *want* to do this, I really want to tell the stories of these people who have been an indispensable part of my life for years now. Have faith in that. You won't be disappointed."

Andy smiled, and sanctioned my grant. "We trust you, your judgment and your work."

* * *

Step one had been taken successfully. A longer road lay ahead, and as soon as I reached India I got down to work. My creative journey was just about to take off.

The task began with elaborate conceptualization and planning, after which the creative artist in me took on a life of his own. The photographer and writer were wakened, and itch to go out and capture the stories of SEWA members in as vivid and fascinating a manner as possible.

As a part of my strategy, I worked out a title for the project first, so the work I did could be aligned with a theme. I thought long and hard. I revisited my entire SEWA experience like a video montage in my head. I tried to discern the most striking and distinctive visual features in all I had witnessed. A few intense imaginative experiences later, I zeroed in on 'hands' as the most visually striking aspect of the people I had worked with, representative of the hard, manual work which defined their lives and existence.

Another distinctive feature, though more abstract, was the courage and optimism displayed in the face of abject poverty and adverse conditions. The desire to work towards improvement and better living conditions, for the sake of their children, not themselves. Collating these thought-threads, I arrived at my title – 'Hands of Hope – Visible Voices from the SEWA Movement'.

Once the central theme and title had been figured out, I sat down to pick some sub-themes, a far easier task.

The project was approved in May 2007, and I was hoping to launch the exhibition and book in March 2008. There was no time to lose.

* * *

Next up was the actual ground work. I travelled extensively to click pictures and get my perfect shots. Photography took me to Bihar, West Bengal, Rajasthan, Madhya Pradesh, Gujarat, and various parts of Delhi. All this travel happened on a very tight timeline. I discovered I enjoyed working like this.

I had been engaged with beneficiaries, employees, and members of SEWA for many years, but the journey as a photographer added new dimensions to my understanding of their lives and their challenges. The world does appear different from behind a camera; you're now a beholder, meditating on what you're seeing, from a distance.

* * *

On a rather warm day early in September, on a trip for the project to a tribal village called Jalsakra in Bihar's Munger district, I was running high fever. I popped two pills on the way and was anxious; I couldn't afford illness. The tightly planned schedule left no room for sickness and rest. Tickets had been booked, and I couldn't miss a single day of work. More importantly, the women in all these locations had been informed in advance of my visit and I absolutely did not want to disappoint them.

I reached Jalsakra feverish and exhausted from continuous travel. I was greeted with the sight of village women carrying heavy bundles of firewood from the forest to their homes. Neither worry nor exhaustion manifested on their faces.

Raji-ben, aged sixty, had just returned with firewood from the forest ten kilometers away from the village. She was carrying a twenty-five kilo load on her head, which she put down to chat with me. After speaking with her for a while, and receiving the kind hospitality of the village, I forgot all about fever, pain, and exhaustion. I was up and about in no time, inspired by the strength of the women in front of me.

* * *

In Munger I met another inspiring woman–Krishna-ben. Her story is painful, but very telling. Her husband died some time ago. In addition to immense grief, this turn of events put her under grave financial stress. She was entitled to a one-time widow's pension payment of 10,000 rupees. The meagerness of the amount is bad enough; the struggle women like her have to go through to procure what they are lawfully entitled to is infinitely worse. Krishna-ben had to run from pillar to post for over a month, submitting her request to block officers for the pension. Her condition was miserable; her request deserved efficient and compassionate attention. Our corruption-ridden system, however, does not treat humans with humanity. They are treated as opportunities to fill private coffers. Krishna-ben's is a case in point.

My eyes welled up when I heard how she had to give half the pension to the Block Development Officer and other staff members. What this officer was developing, I was loathe to understand. How, on what grounds, in what universe can such an act be justified? How does greed overrule human emotion, empathy, and decency to such an extent? I couldn't get it. I knew this practice was rampant – a rule rather than exception – but it was still violently, physically painful to hear her story.

* * *

My travels kept unearthing stories, and aspects of humanity (or the lack thereof) for me. I also got a chance to connect and create new relationships even with people I had known a long time. Consider Jamila-ben of Murshidabad, West Bengal, who was a long-time acquaintance, but took to calling me beta, son, only after I sat with her for a long time, listening to her story.

Another story which shook and shattered me was of that of Rukan, a bidi-roller, again from Murshidabad. With four children at home and a husband away for work in Kolkata, she was finding it difficult to make ends meet. Left with no choice, she had to borrow from a private moneylender. In the absence of savings and a poor inflow of income, she eventually had to sell the bricks off her house to repay the loan. Her house had to be broken brick by brick to keep the hearth running. And there are innumerable such instances, around us every day. We don't have to travel miles to encounter these stories; open your eyes wider to your immediate world and you'll find a plethora to wrench and break your heart right under your nose.

* * *

During the photography journey, I also learned just what a hard form of labor salt farming is. Mukta-ben is a salt farmer in Surendra Nagar district of Gujarat, located in little Rann of Kutch, a six-hour drive from Ahmedabad. After a point there is no road and one has to pass through a stretch of barren land to reach these salt farms. One couldn't reach the precise spot without help from locals, so regional organizers of SEWA accompanied me.

When we arrived, Mukta-ben was asleep in her derelict makeshift shelter, made of dry bushes and bamboo. Mukta-ben was suffering from a high fever and body-ache, and didn't have any medicines to treat her condition. The nearest doctor or dispensary was forty kilometers away, and she couldn't travel that distance all by herself, especially given her weakness and ill-health.

Fortunately, I was carrying some emergency medicines which she could use. After she had rested and felt a bit better, we talked.

Mukta-ben and her husband spent six to eight months in these salt farms surrounded by barren land, fifty kilometers from her own village. This is their only means to eke out a living for themselves and to ensure a future for their children. The work was of course not ideal, but there weren't many employment opportunities in her village.

In her crumbling shelter an old torch, a small radio, and some utensils were her possessions and companions. Even in such drab and dire circumstances, I didn't hear Mukta-ben complaining. She seemed content even while surviving in extreme poverty. Her courage was otherworldly.

* * *

Each of the SEWA members I met while photographing their lives were inspiring, and they remain in my thoughts. Their work, struggles, and small successes keep them optimistic and grounded; their aspirations for the next generation keep them motivated. They have mastered the key to be content with little. Most women I met were very particular about the education of their daughters, so they wouldn't have to struggle like their mothers in this man's world. I myself vacillated between being supremely happy and humbled.

I have never liked the way poverty and the lives of the poor are portrayed in pictures. A sense of misery and helplessness clouds those compositions. The poor are seen as great subjects to evoke pity – and that is all. Yes, they were subjects for me too, but I sought to share their capacities, courage and contribution to the economy. They are silent, invisible, but consistent contributors to our lives. Unrecognized, unthanked. How many of us have so much as wondered who is laboring to make our daily sprinkle of salt available? This simple commodity demands that a woman like Mukta leave her village for eight months, labor under the harshest of conditions, stay in ramshackle shelters, burn her skin, and yet carry on. Incense, papads, embroidery – you name it and there will be a human being living in poverty-stricken conditions, toiling away somewhere in the country under poor light and for a poorer income to create things we use as a matter of mundane privilege.

One of the main intentions of 'Hands of Hope' was to make these women and their efforts visible. The exhibition and the book turned into great tools for advocacy, and did inspire some empathy in the urban ignorant.

* * *

Once I was armed with great stills my next step was to acquire prints and find a venue to display them at. I went about looking for curators to organize the exhibition. To my chagrin, I realized that places like IHC and the Indian International Centre, Delhi's premier cultural venues, are booked months in advance. The curators, too, weren't an easy bunch, requiring high fees and with inflexible conditions of association. Many looked to exploit a newcomer in the field.

Finally, I met someone interesting and straightforward: my colleague Sapna Desai introduced me to Milan Moudgill. Upon seeing my work, he asked, "Are you interested in highlighting the lives of these women, or establish yourself as a photographer?" This was a no-brainer. Of course my purpose was the former.

His teammate, Divya, who was to finally design the exhibition, was also accompanying him. They suggested that we add a little text-story to the pictures to give more relevance and meaning to each for the observer. They were against framing the pictures – the visuals needed to be bare, approachable, and the audience must be able to have a dialogue with them. Moreover, framed text would not look well. I agreed.

The next task was to get the book designed and printed. I had already completed the writing, and in time found able help to both design and print the book. On one hand the photos were coming alive in print, and on the other, this book was becoming a physical reality. I was stunned with disbelief, and thrilled. Until recently I wouldn't have dared to call myself a writer or a photographer. Yet here we were, and I had performed both those roles well enough for public consumption, and driven by a genuinely good cause.

Good intentions and corresponding action, combined with the support of the SEWA Bharat community, the UK partner organization, and continued encouragement from umpteen people including Renana-ben made it possible.

* * *

The exhibition was first launched at the Trade Union Congress office in London on the 8th of March, 2008, followed by a month-long showing at the House of Commons. Back home in India, the book and the exhibition, both titled 'Hands of Hope', were launched at the Mati Ghar in the Indira Gandhi National Centre for Arts on the 15th of March, 2008, and were greeted with an overwhelmingly positive response.

Among the many people who turned up for the inauguration were the women who featured in the pictures and in the book. It was a joyous moment for them too. Hands of Hope was entirely about them, after all. Among the several dignitaries, the known and unknown people who visited the exhibition, I most looked forward to seeing Ela-ben. She looked around keenly, and went directly to the Visitors' Book: "Shabash Sanjay bhai. We all, SEWA sisters, are proud of you!"

Ela-ben Bhatt also authored the foreword for our photo book. Her words carry remarkable wisdom, as well as encouragement and kindness. I am eternally grateful for her presence and support.

Equally significant at the inauguration was the presence of my mother. She travelled all the way from Katihar to be a part of this moment. Her sense of pride was evident. My father had passed away some time ago, but I knew he too would have been proud of my work. It was he who trusted me as I took my first jittery steps in the social sector. "I trust you and I am sure you will do well," he had said. There are no words for my gratitude.

* * *

A string of exhibitions followed the first two. One World Action UK, procured the prints of the photographs so they could organize the exhibition in multiple locations. The photos were exhibited at the DFID (Department for International Development) Headquarters, the Osborne Art Gallery in London, and in South Africa. Closer to home, the photos found an audience at the NCPA (National Centre for the Performing Arts) (Mumbai), Bharat Bhavan (Bhopal), National School of Design (Ahmedabad) and IHC (India Habitat Centre) and IIC (India International Centre) (both in Delhi). The photos continued travelling, to cities like Kolkata, Patna, and Jaipur, as well as others. The exhibition made much noise in the media as well, introducing more people to the purpose behind it.

The Hands of Hope project was successful in every way. It met all initial objectives, and accomplished more. The success of the project made me appreciate action anew. Learning can only happen by doing. When I was young a camera was out of reach. When I got older, possibilities came my way and I grasped them with both hands. The canvas of my imagination was flexible and expansive, even if resources were initially not. Once again, I cannot emphasize enough that there is never only one route to anything. I was able to pursue a latent passion, and publish the stories of women workers all over the country, stories of inspiration, courage, and struggle, all through a single project. This, because I refused to dismiss either as a priority.

The final takeaway from this episode again, was that you are never alone in your successes. A number of factors and people need to be aligned to make things dazzle. This time the blessings of the entire SEWA community powered me. The wave of creativity which got unleashed had them as its source. My contribution was simply to channel their narratives.

❑❑

Chapter Nine

Meditation

Chandrashekhar Jha was an intelligent and intuitive man. He didn't just read horoscopes, he was adept at reading the minds of people. At the time of our meeting, through a mutual friend in 2002, he would have been about 27 or 28. We were both Biharis – a common belonging became analogous with a common understanding.

Chandrashekhar began his practice early in life, and had an enviable clientele, including ministers and celebrities. I am not sure if Rahul - our mutual friend - continued pursuing his astrological advice, but I became a great fan of Chandrashekhar's. The first time we met he predicted I would go abroad soon and should be ready with my passport. I went to Netherlands for a short diploma course. Seema and I both started consulting him regularly. He also prescribed some stones, which I began wearing as rings. These stones were supposed to have positive effects on aspects of life one wished was enhanced, and were similarly capable of subduing negative 'tendencies'. Very quickly, we were visiting him more than we did any temple. Telephone consultations were frequent, daily, and we started meeting him socially. He calls me bhaiya. Elder brother.

For any and everything, Chandru, as we fondly took to calling him, was just a call away. Chandru didn't fix our problems or magic away our anxieties; they are a part and parcel of existence. But he became a figure to appeal to, a sounding board, a rock.

* * *

In 2009, life suddenly seemed to stagnant. Nothing new was coming my way - and I suppose after the flurry and the success of the photography exhibition I came to expect or wish for novelty, for a different kind of tempo. Daily work became a grind. Complacency snuck into life, and negativity, something that resembled contempt. I had started feeling dissatisfied with my work and fatigued with similar, repetitive tasks. I felt there was no scope for innovation, and no challenge in life.

In retrospect, I was ripe for the kind of faith that becomes a crutch. In retrospect, I simply missed what I had always been aware of - that the momentum of a creative project like Hands of Hope had been decades of consistent work and little sparks of daily, obscure imaginings in the making.

Amid this chaos, our daughter Tathya came into our lives. She was a welcome change for both Seema and for me – her tender presence and her pleasant cackles filled our lives with warmth and joy.

The feeling of professional insipidness persisted, though. It was the same work, the same people, the same programs, and the same routines – a rigmarole I wished to escape from, and found difficult to see any differently. What I was feeling is not unique: burnout is common in the social sector. The work is unending and thankless except in transitory, individual ways. The same problem is solved over, and over, and over again, and yet finds another victim, and another, and another. Staying powerful too becomes a weapon against oneself - tenacity becomes a personal code, a point of private pride, and permits no rest. I was unable to balance professional frustrations with personal commitments. I wasn't giving adequate attention to my family, and to my newborn. This disrupted our peace at home, causing daily stress and tension. Seema and the kids were by no means responsible for my distress, yet they bore the brunt of it. Squabbles between partners are not rare, but perpetual disagreement does distort the harmony necessary for a healthy home-life and have a negative impact on children's minds. I was aware of this, felt terribly guilty and unhappy, and was yet helpless. No matter how hard I tried life seemed to be racing downhill.

Professional lows can be explained, quantified, and analysed. But psychic conflicts cannot be understood or delineated without the kind of help societies all over the world stigmatize, and which is hard to find in India anyway. Therapy might have helped - but I had Chandru. My being had become a battleground. I seemed to have lost control over my emotions, my responses and behaviours, my motivations and priorities. There seemed no oasis of peace or solace in sight – neither work, nor family seemed a haven. I was fighting internal battles on a daily, hourly basis, and losing them all.

Just when I felt I was on the verge of a breakdown, I was introduced to Jagadish Manjhi. Acharya Jagadish Manjhi is a retired Professor of Psychology and was trained in the practice of meditation by Shri Shri Anandamurti and Professor Indradev Gupta.

Just as calling up Chandru and consulting him began to feel like a daily chore, like a dependency, like I was held captive and couldn't take any decisions independently, I learned how to meditate.

Meditation has been celebrated as a panacea by many before me; it is also ridiculed as hogwash akin to my stone rings. The difference between the two is vital: astrology required me to pay money to an external mediator between me and my stars; meditation required me simply to pay attention, to what I already knew, what my mind and my body were shouting through my psychological anguish and my physiological exhaustion. In the words of its own discourse, meditation is a science that teaches concentration and expansion, of one's consciousness. Our mind, a unit of cosmic energy, is inherently distractable. Meditation helps us bring the scattered pieces of the mind together. It also facilitates awareness of just how far this mind can expand. The internal journey of the mind that withdraws temporarily from the material world can be spectacular. By focusing on our selves with an objective inner eye, we can view the neuroses we are burdened with as irrelevant on the larger scale we are concentrating on. The relief this provides allows our minds to still and heal.

Practically speaking, once you start expanding your mind and your consciousness, you can apply yourself to think bigger and accomplish greater goals. And yes, this is precisely what meditation helped me achieve.

* * *

The charm of astrology wore off quickly once I started talking to myself more than spoke to Chandru. Meditation compelled me to explore my strengths and weaknesses. This resuscitated some of my dwindling confidence. By creating an internal site of peace, meditation also helped me slowly achieve greater harmony with my surroundings.

Acharya Jagadish's classes on meditation theory touched on theories of evolution, karma-karmafal or action and consequence, curiosity, and the journey of the mind through memory and awareness. These classes were invariably unique and fulfilling. They were always held in modest venues, some in Katihar. The expense of organizing classes, food, and venue rental was divided amongst participants; we generally paid a nominal amount. The entire exercise was simple, and reinforced our belief in simplicity as a value.

A further liberating principle of meditation was that the teacher is merely a facilitator, sharpening comprehension. This relief from a medium, an intermediary to the experience of understanding oneself and what one does or should value has reminded me repeatedly of every religious reformation in history: organised religions (and belief systems like astrology) have a tendency to gravitate toward dogma, and then to appoint and exorbitantly empower its arbiters, its guardians. In our time, in Bihar as well as in other parts of this country, those with fanatic psuedo-loyalty to symbols and artificially puffed-up hatred of Others have lost all sense of perspective, all sense of what is humanly important in life. The reason is precisely this - that they have no accessible connection whatsoever with their own selves as miniscule parts of an infinite whole, no more or less than their fellows. All they see and hear in their confusion is an external symbol, an external representative of 'us' who asks his followers to repudiate a politically convenient 'them', and they most violently do.

Meditation is different. You do not need anyone to pray; you do not even need someone to pray to. There is no prescribed time or place. You do not need an idol, a manual, or a photograph to be connected to the unspoken unspeaking supreme consciousness.

* * *

During our interactions Acharya Jagadish and I discussed potential and possibilities, and how meditation can play a constructive role in harnessing potential. Each revelation was a new spark, enlivening my verve for life. Talking to Acharya Jagadish became a means to understanding my self.

My journey into the self was a journey into defining meaning, structuring an accessing positivity, self-actualization, and into mindfulness. The principle social accompaniment of meditation amused me: do no harm. I was after all fulfilling my parents' ambitions for me too, albeit in an unexpected and unconventional way.

Meditation was a dive deep into the soul, the atman. I spent hours exploring my self, my behaviour patterns in an objective way. It became easier for me to see what mistakes I was repeatedly making, and understanding when and how I was hurting others, even involuntarily; I began to see instances of my own irrational behaviour. Meditation neither does nor promises to magically vanquish aspects of your personality or 'teach' you right action, but it impel you to recognize and accept wherever you've gone wrong. It does minimize your tendency to destructive or counter productive behaviour, because your being grows ever fuller of positive energy. Negative emotions are checked by reinvigorated perspective.

Meditation also helped me understand the behaviour of those around me too. People act in accordance with their natures, their conditioning, their experiences and habit. Meditation is leisure, mental and physical, to appreciate the lives of others. One becomes more observant, understanding, and compassionate.

I missed my father sorely after his demise, his gentle guidance and his ability to always voice reason and encouragement in the direst times. Acharya Jagadish too fulfilled a like role in my life. He, in fact, bestowed a lovely name on my daughter – Tathya – essence, meaning, fact.

Seema and I grew to love meditation. And a kind of harmony, peace, and balance were restored to our household.

* * *

Meditation has continued to infuse my daily life and everyday interactions and response to challenges with calm and confidence. Through the difficult years of sameness, as well as through the dizzyingly alien, full and active year at Harvard, meditation helped both Seema and I stay grounded, focused on our respective goals, our material and financial condition, and our priorities.

* * *

In time Acharya Jagadish suggested he might groom me as an Acharya in my turn. This required continued and rigorous application, and training others in the practice. The intense sessions that followed are, I feel certain, responsible for the stupendous amount I was able to accomplish at work, my focus and fiercely channelled energy. The mind used to err sometimes, but I was able to control my mental capacities better.

I also gave up animal flesh. It is difficult, in fact, to reconcile one's awareness of and feeling of oneness with the environment, kinship with life, and continue to kill and consume fellow beings. It began to feel gory and unsettling.

I completed my training shortly before leaving for the US. I knew I had to teach, but the true challenge was knowing an Acharya is meant to lead by example. My words and gestures, my actions, beliefs, and observations must carry particular weight, have significance to me, so they might be useful to others, I must be willing to be seen, and to be emulated. I must take responsibility for those who sought my guidance.

Cambridge predominantly offered non-vegetarian food. Harvard especially, offered few alternatives to meat and we resorted perforce to more economical homecooked food. Chaitanya and Tathya continued omnivorous; such life choices, I think, are best left to one's self.

* * *

I offered up meditation for the first time in Professor Heifetz's Leadership classes. During a discussion on 'Finding Sanctuary for the Self', I spoke passionately about the constructive role meditation can play in increasing self-awareness, and offered to train students in techniques.

Ladan, a Parsi friend from Washington D.C was the first to show interest, followed by Latica, another good friend hailing from Croatia. A string of trainees followed, all from different parts of the globe – Ruixi and Cathy from China; Akbar from Texas; Patty from Peru; Vidhi and Jeenal from India... I was delighted to have brought not only myself but this fruitful technique around the world: from the hinterlands to Bihar to the suave columns of Harvard. Its appeal and application seemed universally valuable, and I continued to reach out to people.

I have continued to teach meditation back in India too. People have always approached me for counsel or simply to share pressing issues. I always enjoyed these conversations and contributed the best I could. Now, talking to, guiding, and counselling people facing dilemmas, distress or doubt, is a responsibility. Being able to offer solace is a joy - but I am newly aware of the effect I might have. Listening to someone is not equivalent with solving their problems, but it is important to offer comfort and help folks put things in perspective.

Meditation has helped harmonize my inner and outer worlds, and left my existence in a far more stable state than it ever was before.

❑❑

Chapter Ten

Giving Back to Katihar

I had left Katihar with a sweet and bitter memories, but my sense of belonging to the place was steadfast. Most of us who wander out venture to many places, not finding anchor in any one location. However, my attachment to Katihar and the people here kept me anchored, and the notion that I have a place to return to, alive. My people are waiting for me here. Katihar lived onward in my mind. I can rattle off names of shops, eating joints, photo studios, garment stores, and every conceivable Katihar landmark even today. I even remember each immortal and unchanging speedbreaker.

I have always consciously worked on staying in touch with people. Memories and nostalgia of childhood often assailed me. I still felt connected to the streets, the markets, my school, the playground and my favourite nooks. I was perpetually homesick for the first few years. My face would light up at the thought of visiting Katihar, and my heart burdened with sudden grief each I time I stepped into Katihar Railway Station to board a train back to Delhi. I know my mother cried for hours after my departure. And the strange feeling of leaving my father's safe, secure, and humbling shade was always palpable. Some friends would come see me off, and their companionship was a solace even in their absence, later.

My association with Katihar is stronger than words can say: people, place, and culture.

* * *

Katihar formed a subconscious backdrop and the reference point for all my experiences outside it. I compared new people, their habits and amenities, to those in Katihar, always acutely aware of how much needed to be done back home. Katihar had people and potential, but any transformation of physical, lived conditions requires a change in mindset, a break from age-old traditions and a yen for future possibilities. Katihar is traditionalist: this was the greatest challenge.

I had been involved with grassroots work in several semi-urban and rural districts at SEWA. Our organization was active in Munger and Bhagalpur, but I had deliberately avoided taking any initiative in Katihar till I was very sure. I wanted the demand to come from the locals, especially from women. Along with a need assessment by SEWA, this alone could create the organizational push necessary to effect change in Katihar.

When we were working with incense stick rollers in Munger we faced a sudden roadblock: a rapid hike in the price of raw materials. This impacted the viability of our business model. To avert further crisis, we were advised to consider involving women in bamboo production; it is a key raw material. The idea sounded good and we immediately decided to implement it.

Katihar and adjoining areas are known for bamboo. The crisis in Munger became a path to Katihar, where we started a livelihood program with a dual objective – to support incense production in Munger, and to create employment opportunities for the women of Katihar.

Understandably, it was a thrilling turn of events for me, personally. I was going to be in Katihar, giving back to the land that bore and nurtured me.

* * *

Another opportunity arose as work in Katihar continued–A Solid Waste Management Project. This has been a critical issue in rapidly developing sites, where the infrastructure for waste management is either non-existent, or inadequate to meet the needs of a growing population. Trash dumps spilling over into inhabited areas, and garbage dumps on streets, common grounds, and drains is a common sight across India. The accompanying stench and lack of hygiene has been accepted as a cost of urbanization. The problem of waste disposal has become all the more severe because the huge plastic component of waste just doesn't decompose. In towns like Katihar, extremely toxic waste from industries and nursing homes also acts as an environmental and health hazard. This piling waste is destroying community spaces and the general well-being of society.

What is the individual to do in this situation? Most citizens pay taxes, so expect municipal authorities to deal with urban governance and infrastructure development. Yet individual accountability is as important - toward reducing waste generation if nothing else. But the work of municipal corporations does in any case fall miles short of expectations and necessity. Apathetic authorities and complacent citizens – the situation makes for a vicious system which doesn't allow progressive measures to be instituted promptly.

* * *

The government of India published the Solid Waste Management Rules in 2000 and instructed municipal corporations to explore opportunities of partnership with civil society organizations and private companies to manage waste. Generally, the tendering process is designed to favor big companies, which exclude the waste picking and cleaning communities. In 2011, an international development agency offered us operation of a pilot waste management project in Bihar that intended an experiment with an alternate waste management model that involved communities and not companies.

I couldn't stop myself suggesting we conduct the pilot in Katihar. The task was difficult, but I was confident that I would manage it well in my own town, as I was familiar with people of influence and local administrative nitty-gritties. I forgot that two decades had elapsed since I took my first train ride out of Katihar. The culture and context had changed, but I was ready, even excited, to finally have an opportunity to pay my place back meaningfully.

* * *

Even local politics had changed. I had dived headfirst into Katihar carrying this big project, with no realization that the town was burgeoning, a nascent city. The population had increased manifold, without significant increase in geographic size. Katihar had seen massive migration in from nearby villages, with no new spaces built to accommodate the additional residents. Roads remained narrow, since earlier constructions prohibited expansion. Vehicular movement was painful chaos at best. Organized parking was unheard of. No planning had informed the city's growth; authorities and corporations existed purely to pay lip service to responsibilities and mandates.

This was the stage on which our organization set out to develop an inclusive and effective waste management project for implementation in Katihar. The main objective of this project was to promote employment and reduce poverty among waste pickers, as well as cleaning up the city. Our model was a door-to-door waste collection system that interacted directly with households. Meeting the needs of both our workers and residents, the model aimed at financial sustainability, efficient waste segregation, and recycling.

The idea was excellent, and aimed to fulfil several simultaneous objectives. We planned to organize women waste pickers and cleaners into a cooperative, so they could take over the cleaning and recycling exercise once the project was over. We wanted to prove that the local community of cleaners could do a more efficient job of pan-city waste management than big companies, while also ensuring employment for the poverty-stricken waste pickers, who had no other skill sets.

We also wanted to prove that garbage collection was better managed by segregating waste, dry and kitchen waste, funded by a small monthly contribution received from citizens. We aimed to manage solid waste in such a way that recyclable waste was reused and kitchen waste composted, a much more environmentally sensitive and sustainable process.

The waste management project was a golden opportunity, to help save the city's fast-deteriorating environment and restoring the dignity of the untouchable Dom caste. I had observed the community closely, having spent my childhood literally adjacent to their ghetto on Railway land. I was aware of their abysmal living conditions and of societal apathy towards them. They are known as Mahadalits, their status comparable to the most vulnerable and oppressed sections of Indian society. Any state assistance for them is cosmetic at best. Authorities and officers who are supposed to work for their welfare have a snobbish, cold attitude. The problem of untouchability is real, even in the 21st century - and one requires more than just papers and processes to tackle it. A thorough understanding of the caste's historical rejection, and basic empathy and humanity is imperative to hope for their emancipation. Here was my chance to undertake some concrete work that might just open a window or two in a dim home or two and let in some light.

* * *

We secured funding to support the project from June 2011 through March 2014. In February 2012 we secured a contract with the Katihar Municipal Corporation to implement a pilot on a partnership basis. It was hoped that this model and the lessons it garnered would inform and enrich debates and policy solutions towards developing waste management solutions not just in Bihar, but all across India.

Confident of my plan and intent, I was sure we could deliver on the ground as well. However, when we approached the newly elected councillors and the city mayor, we received a mixed reaction. They had several questions to stall our model – why do you want to charge money when citizens already pay taxes? Making citizens pay more will affect our vote bank! Where would you throw the garbage? What transport would you use? What about citizens unwilling or unable to pay the service fee? What if you falter on your commitment? What about the cleaners already employed by the municipal corporation?

While some of these questions were legitimate, a plethora more were asked simply to demotivate us and throw us off course. It was a few positive and progressive councillors who saw how genuine and thorough we were in our modelling, and who encouraged Katihar Municipal Corporation to try the model out.

What truly turned the Corporation toward us was our assurance that we expected no financial support from them - that we had funding. From dilly-dallying they switched to showing prompt interest and enthusiasm in our project.

Post official sanction we began the project in handpicked municipal wards. The response was favourable. People liked the idea of a women's cooperative collecting and managing solid waste. Once we had citizen support, we gradually convinced the Corporation to contribute a portion of the finances so we could expand our network. They agreed to contribute 30 percent of the total project cost for nine main municipal wards in the town area, while we continued to run the operation from our own funds for two. The Citizens hugely demanded to continue the project. We were soon implementing the integrated solid waste management project successfully in eleven wards.

* * *

I wish I could say work with such noble intentions and positive environmental and social impact continued unabated and grew from strength to strength. However, hiccups are part of participating in India's governance framework, even as a mere civil society partner.

As soon as the Corporation became a funding partner, the insidious and unforeseen obstacles started cropping up. When we cleared drains blocked for a mind-boggling two decades or so, municipal staff members choked its other end. Councillors expected us to clean marriage ceremony sites before and after the function without payment. Others were perpetually dissatisfied with our work, finding invisible flaws even as the citizenry extended their full support. Not altogether surprising, but it seemed the councillors had assumed a personal grudge against us, simply because were more efficient at what was meant to be their job! They hated losing control over the waste pickers and the cleaning community, and were hell-bent on maintaining the status quo.

A little digging revealed too the core source of their hostility towards us was an expectation of monetary favours. The

Corporation and the councillors were expecting cash in return for their cooperation. It was an abnormal scenario, we learned later, that the Corporation was footing 30 percent of the cost without any commission or cut. A fairly well-organized system of distributing this commission exists within the Corporation. For every payment from the Corporation for construction, 10 percent of the billed amount was supposed to go towards the *unofficially designated person* who acted as a liaison. Thereafter, the amount was distributed among the office bearers, ranging from 1.5 percent to the Assistant Engineer, 1 percent for the Executive Engineer, 1 percent to the Accountant and office staff, 1 percent to the Mayor, 1 percent for the CEO, 0.5 percent to the Deputy Mayor, 1 percent for the Superintending Engineer, and so on and so forth. The Commissioner got the same amount as the Mayor and the highest, 3 percent, was handed over to the Junior Engineer who took the greatest risk, signing official documents and statements.

In case of purchases and supplies, the commission is 20 percet to 30 percent, and the Mayor, the Commissioner and a few other key officials take big chunks home since no Engineer is involved in the process.

This elaborate set up sounds like a thrilling fictional plot, but the malignancy in our system is real. This was my first first-hand experience of the nittie-gritties I thought I had known. Evidence is hard to come by; the avaricious officials have created a fool-proof system for taking cuts and siphoning off funds, but many locals confirm the practices persist.

* * *

The fundamental principles of our organization were clear. We remained non-committal in the face of any extra payment or commission. We were happy to provide learning support to the Corporation members, and organized several exposure visits for the Mayor, the councillors and the administrative team. We even took the district administration team including the CEO of the municipal corporation on a city-exposure tour to Ahmedabad. After this exposure, the CEO was finally convinced of our sincerity and our work, and decided to *officially* partner with us.

Conversations around bribery were never loud, but covert attempts at extracting money from us were continuous. Eventually, the Mayor and his team withdrew their support. A leading national daily that extolled our work, reported on administrative hostility we faced: "A section of municipal officials, aggrieved at being denied their monthly cut, got the earlier sanitation workers to repeatedly dump the foulest form of garbage in the main public square every time the saathis (SEWA waste pickers) would clean it, once notably to mar the visit of then Deputy Chief Minister Sushil Kumar Modi to Katihar".

We also managed to send councillors to see waste and urban management techniques used in bigger Indian cities. I even took the Mayor to Naples, Italy, in 2012 to participate in and talk during the 6th Session of the World Urban Forum. Unfortunately, neither the Councillors nor the Mayor showed any inclination to learn anything productive from the visits; their single-minded focus was on sight-seeing and recreation. The situation was frustrating and disheartening, but my resolution remained strong – to put Katihar on the world map for cleanliness and for our unique model of solid-waste management through organizing a waste pickers collective.

As long as we got funding and support from an international foundation - that is, till 2014 - the work continued uninterrupted. For the duration, 150 poverty stricken women and men from the most vulnerable socio-economic sections had a regular income. They acquired dignity after being cast out of society through their lives. Their service was recognized for the value it added to the city. Citizens participated in the project by regularly paying their user fee.

Things changed when the international fund ran dry. We approached the Mayor and his team to renew our contract and pay us to continue the project, but he was openly hostile. Bad-mouthing of our efforts began. The message was loud and clear – since no money was flowing in, we weren't wanted any longer.

The Corporation opened tenders to invite new contractors on board. A few Councillors tried to approach me clandestinely, and crack new deals behind closed doors. I was invited to a hotel room by two rather late at night. Desperate to keep the project running, I went, even though part of me anticipated the worst. Fortunately Sanjeev, a good friend, had accompanied me. Three people welcomed me into the room. I knew two of them well, and the third, the stranger was carrying a pistol. A cold sweat broke on my forehead. I was trapped.

It was this third person who talked. The councillors could perhaps not verbalize their proposal and expectations openly, not least because we were well acquainted with each other. The armed man said, "The leader of the Corporation will face a no-confidence motion in two years. He will need to buy votes and will need cash to secure his position. You can understand there is tremendous pressure on him to acquire funds for his own security and the waste management contract is an important opportunity to do this. Why act foolish? Think about his situation. Inflate the cost and accept a chunk for yourself. Make this a win-win situation for all." He made it sound very matter of fact, as if it was the most natural course of affairs in the world. "If the elections and motion go per plan, you will benefit a lot too. Think about it, and reconsider your stand."

I was scared, but my and SEWA's answer was clear and unchanged. They knew it too. I left the hotel room saying this was against our conscience and philosophy.

This stand was harder to execute even than to take. I knew many waste pickers would lose their livelihoods. They would have to withdraw their children from school and make peace with being relegated to the invisible margins again. My conscience, however, was clear and the principles of my organization sound. The insensitive greed festering in the hearts of these councillors did make me sick. My very soul wept at the impunity with which they sought a slice out of the livelihoods of people subsisting on crumbs.

It was time to leave Katihar. Renewing the contract with the Corporation was not feasible. Also, I was shortly due to leave for Harvard. There was nothing more to do here, not now. I was leaving Katihar empty-handed. I had undertaken this journey from Katihar to Delhi several times, but never had my heart felt as wounded as it did today.

* * *

Optimism, positive stubbornness, has persisted in me even through the darkest hours. My friend and valued informal advisor Vikash provided me lot of emotional support, but always remained sceptical of support from the stakeholders in this project. I still kept in touch with the Mayor and the Corporation even while I was in Harvard, repeatedly assuring them that no other organization would be able to deliver the results we had. The contract was awarded to another organization, and the avaricious councillors became hidden partners ensuring the in-flow to their pockets ran unhindered even if the drains remained clogged. Our three and half year long diligence went in vain. The corrupt system managed to defeat us.

This particular initiative was altruistic in its very essence. It sought to empower the most vulnerable through a sustainable livelihood. Their earning more than doubled due to the project – from Rs 1500 or 2000 it went up to Rs 4500 per month. These figures sound miniscule to many, but the increase helped the waste pickers send their children to school, buy household goods, and even repay old loans.

We called them 'Soundarya Saathi' because that is what they were – our partners in helping beautify the city. Historically denounced as untouchables, this was a landmark initiative helping them win dignity and start inhabiting mainstream society, even in a small capacity. Their services opened the eyes of people to the value they add to urban living. People were dependent on them for ensuring disease-free, sanitary habitation, and this realization helped them earn much-needed respect.

Even this kind of initiative presented many challenges; holding the waste pickers collective together was the biggest. Despite our best efforts, there was little sense of togetherness: the collective constantly threatened to break down. The first, larger faction, comprised 80 percent of the members - mostly women. The other, comprising 20 percent of the members - mostly men - felt dissatisfied with the emoluments and benefits. They were loyal above all to their caste broker – a sort of local caste leader who doubled as a moneylender for the community, and again as a power-broker between the Corporation and this poverty-ridden, illiterate populace. They hailed him as a messiah. In fact he had a vested interest in disrupting our work: he was providing loans at exorbitant interest rates, taking advantage of borrowers in desperate circumstances. The exploiter made his victims dependent on him, and enjoyed unlimited power in all their affairs. The caste broker constantly sought to create disharmony in the community for political benefit to himself. His booze and cash ruined any chance for our group to achieve a sustainable internal equilibrium. Even people with common vulnerabilities can be divided if short-term benefits are dangled in front of them.

Before becoming part of our programme, the waste pickers were not organized, had meagre incomes and no place to go to for financial assistance. None of them had a bank account. Through our initiative they set up a credit cooperative. We also worked on issues like health and education: the self-sufficiency implied threatened the caste-broker-cum-moneylender. He claimed to serve the welfare of his folks, but power intoxicated him. When he couldn't buy loyalty, he resorted to physical abuse. For two years he tried and failed to get them to toe his line, and then went completely on the offensive with open threats to their lives. The self-proclaimed emancipator's actual villainous colours were emerging for everyone to see.

He had been mobilizing the regular municipal cleaners during festivals each year, and had them cast himself as their leader too. He negotiated on behalf with the Corporation for improved wages - and took a commission per person, along with a sizeable lump sum from the increment as a whole. He tried to employ the same tactic with us. During the festive period in 2012, he mobilized the workers of the municipal corporation to go on a strike, bringing the work to a complete halt. In October, when the workers were on strike, the Deputy Chief Minister of the state was due to visit Katihar to inaugurate the new Corporation building. Our members were not a part of the strike, but the caste-broker was trying his best to forcefully rope them in. The District Magistrate came to our rescue, and filed a written complaint against him.

But the seed of discord had been sowed. Some of our members threatened to go on strike just before the festival season, demanding increased and advance salary, as well as a bonus. It created disequilibrium within our setup and generated immense mistrust between team members.

Around the same time, we were planning to register a Cooperative for the cleaners so they could run the program themselves. We never intended to build an employer-employee relationship with the waste pickers. Our intent was to empower the community. Luckily, I was physically present in the town when the mayhem broke. I decided to intervene personally and have a chat with the members. It took several rounds of calm and reasoned dialogue to convey the many benefits of the program for the participants' sustenance and future. I exhorted them to not be myopic. I also managed to present at the initiative as their own program. They decided to no go on strike.

The cycle repeated itself in October 2013. The broker targeted the male members first, with whose help he forced the women into submission. The women were threatened with beatings if they refused to participate in the strike. When the situation came to my notice I called an emergency meeting with the women members. I explained, honestly, that we lacked the funds to meet their demands. They were very understanding, and by now they had started reaping the benefits of our program. They were able to send their children to school, managed at least some savings for the future with the help of their stable incomes. Emboldened by their support, I encouraged them to come to work the next morning, assuring them of my presence in case anything untoward happened.

Around fifty women and a few men turned up early in the morning, around 6 am, and I encouraged them to begin the cleaning work. All went well for a while, till a group of fifteen or twenty men appeared out of nowhere to disrupt our work. These men told our members to immediately stop work. I immediately intervened and politely asked them to leave. The work continued. The men started throwing the collected garbage all over the place, creating a violent ruckus. All of this was happening right in the heart of the city, in Mangal Bazaar. The situation seemed to be completely out of control and I would be lying if I didn't admit I feared our entire program would crumble then and there.

I collected myself and called the police. In their classic apathetic tone, they asked me to manage on my own!

I then called up a lawyer friend. Coincidentally, the broker and he had studied together and knew each other fairly well. I had avoided meeting with the caste-broker for about two years, but at the insistence of the lawyer friend we decided to meet immediately. He wanted to talk in front of all the members and put forth the same old demands. I responded, calmly, that we did not have enough funds to afford a bonus, but we could give them half a month's salary in advance. The flaring conflagration was thus controlled but not all glowing embers cooled. A few of his accomplices continued to trouble us, all but unmanageable even on their own.

* * *

If dealing with community leaders was difficult, nothing could prepare us for the shocks we would receive dealing with officials of the state government.

As I said before, one of our main objectives was to register a cooperative of women waste pickers, so they could eventually run the show on their own. For this, we had to approach the state-run Cooperative Department. Predictably, this department refused to cooperate with us when we filed our registration request. They deliberately provided us with wrong information about registration procedures so we had to redo our application thrice. And even when we got everything right the file simply wouldn't move up! The way to fast-track affairs was the same – slide some money into relevant pockets and see the file fly forward. The inspector actually asked one of our colleagues to 'at least' buy him two kilos of mangoes in lieu of a bribe! This was said with utter nonchalance.

No one was interested in working for the welfare of those who most deserved our empathy. The state government was responsible for framing a solid waste policy, a work in progress then. Our project was being closely monitored to gather data, understand outcomes, and embed credible strategies into their own plan. None of them, however, thought of extending any help to us.

City dwellers had never managed solid waste on their own and were completely dependent on the authorities. Many threw garbage onto the streets or into empty lots around their homes. The city government was least concerned about attempting institutional changes to tackle this behavior. They kept citing a dearth of cleaners to manage the scale of waste being generated.

When we introduced the concept of inclusive waste management through the door-to-door collection of kitchen waste, citizens liked the idea and gave it their wholehearted support. However, their role remained limited to using the facility and paying the fee, or at most mobilizing their immediate neighbours to participate in this manner. They did not see the need to engage with the issue at large, to have any tough conversations on civic amenities with the municipal corporation. The people could have been our strongest allies, but our local team failed to win less apolitical support from them despite several attempts. There seemed no possibility of collective social action even around such an important subject.

* * *

This phase spent at the grassroots in Katihar jolted me completely. Our intent, work, and model did not have any significant flaw. Our planning was meticulous and our efforts driven by genuine empathy for the marginalized. Personal lust and institutionalized apathy, however, did not let even the noblest intentions thrive. Our model was a moderate success, but our attempt to bring about an overall improvement in the lives of the vulnerable Mahadalits failed.

I had once posted for help on Facebook, engaging Dalit leaders from Delhi, several of them old friends from university. While their ideals were articulate and convincing, no one actually wanted to take the trouble to travel to far-flung areas and actually dirty their hands to bring about change. Delhi is a safe site for dealing caste cards. A few shallow words of support, and the conversations ceased. No one supported the cause openly.

The Corporation and the Mayor – we failed handling both. It took a while for us to understand that our principles and motivations were antithetical, and they couldn't go together. My promise to help place Katihar on the world map was left unfulfilled. This after several small wins. We even hosted the then Country Director of the World Bank and his wife (who was an expert in urban governance herself). They were keen to support our efforts. They journeyed for over 40 hours in a train to reach our town and meet all the key stakeholders. I was sure big things were in motion, but no one seemed to have the foresight and vision to understand them.

I certainly learned something through all this - how important it is to stay engaged and open conversations, even if it invites trouble. I should have been more proactive handling internal disequilibrium and tried harder for timely, amicable solutions.

My eldest brother Arun bhaiya, who probably understood the city better than me, once advised me to "keep a low profile and go slow". Driven by enthusiasm, I didn't pay much attention. But his advice rang through my head again when Professor Heifetz quoted the maxim about moving slower to move faster. I should have been more careful at each step, taking stock and incorporating revisions wherever needed.

I believe we should have gone to court to highlight the corruption in the municipal corporation once our project was shut down. Unfortunately, by the time we could have done so I was already at the Kennedy School and the team didn't feel strong enough to fight the harassment legally in my absence.

When we lost the bid, the waste pickers lost. The citizens had wallowed in dirt earlier and their lives were back to square one. But the ones whose lives really needed change, needed emancipation and illumination – the waste pickers – they were the most adversely affected, by insidious intent and avarice. The citizens would passively blame the authorities, not look within and chastise themselves for lack of social action. Not think that if each one of us decided to return even a minim back to the society, or even become active participants as we ought to be in our local, common good, how much would change.

But the project had already impacted the waste pickers in many positive ways. They were able to eat nutritious food, not subsist on rat-infested grain. Their kids were getting an education. They were saving. They had earned dignity at least in some quarters. The women workers, especially, felt empowered after generations of cloistered, shackled, troubled existence. They still call me up and cry. They share heart-wrenching stories of exploitation by new organizations and plead that I start work with them again.

I cannot, not just yet. My only consolation is that these waste pickers did at least have a chance to experience the difference, for however short a duration. They could at least sift the good from the bad, and distinguish between exploitation and empowerment.

* * *

The experience was disheartening, but my endeavour to give back to Katihar has not ended yet. I left Katihar with a vow that I will come back again after my Harvard year and resume social action from this place, and would scale-up to other parts of Bihar and the country. I was confident that I would be back with more clarity and vigour and would give my best to start work around ever larger issues. I was only leaving the town to come back again.

❑❑

Chapter Eleven

Incidents and Interactions, Shaping Perceptions

Life is a path, as the worn image goes; experiences hold one hand as you walk and lessons clutch the other. I keep harking back to mine, and wish always to pass on.

Some of these lessons were instant realizations, reactions to observations or interactions. Others took time, and I could only arrive at them after spending hours and hours in reverie. Issues that have managed to stir my sensibilities and shock me pertain severally to my family or to myself, but many impact society at large. Most of them are human made, and humans have too the capacity to find solutions for them, but don't. Sometimes from neglect, sometimes for power, issues plaguing the general populace survive for decades. Till something affects those in power personally, it garners little more than general apathy.

I had never been to a Collector's office through childhood. I only got a chance to visit one when my professional career was unfolding. My first official meeting with the Collector's office was in Munger, my second in Murshidabad, followed by one back home in Katihar. Surprising patterns emerged. First, despite a prior appointment, the Collectors were always preoccupied, signing papers and clearing files while the meeting was in progress. Our meetings were accorded parallel, secondary attention, and eye-contact was established only to conclude the discussion. Second, the considerable distance between the Collector's table and the chairs where the visitors sat. This, it seemed, had been maintained to emphasize upon the chasm that existed between the administration and the common man. The head of the administration, the Collector, seems the de facto maalik, owner, of any district.

This deliberate distancing – of the person and her concern - greatly perturbed me. It is a clear hindrance to effective governance - one could even call it feudal. The control which authority figures are wont to exercise on the masses remind one of the British Raj, vestiges of which are still active in Indian bureaucracy. Ironically, Europeans have been able to put far more democratic and accessible systems of administration in place, and we, who vehemently fought off the Raj, are clinging to the power structures it established to distance the filthy native from the superior Sahabs. Our modern Collectors function with the same Sahab complex – they are captive to it.

* * *

I had an interesting encounter with an erstwhile Collector of Katihar. We had been introduced by a senior bureaucrat, so he did his best to give me due attention. Even so, the simultaneous paper signing continued like a sacred ritual. I had gone to him to seek help on the solid waste management project. He was kind enough to order a cup of coffee for me, but he began rambling, oblivious of our agenda for the meeting. He tutored me on the privileges of being a Collector. "You know Sanjay, the SP and MLAs park their vehicles in the porch reserved for me, and I have to instruct my office to have them removed. When will these people understand that a Collector is not just a designation, it is an institution in itself?" This power complex is ingrained in our civil servants. Serving citizens in secondary; supercilious self-congratulation runs foremost on their mind.

In an over-populated country like India, where effective administration is indispensable and the only source of hope for so many, such officers are cause for grave worry. The fear of becoming like them is perhaps why I am glad I didn't pursue the civil services as a career. This is not to say such a superiority complex and such condescension is ubiquitous; there are several graceful exceptions and many with whom I have personal experience with. But without exception, all public offices need to be closer to and less distant from the masses. They should be humanized institutions, with service their core value. This very component - 'service' - is unfortunately missing from most interactions and transactions with the people.

* * *

In our country, politicians enjoy a dubious reputation. They spend time among prospective voters and promise them the stars and the moon when elections are imminent, but after victory, even recognizing the faces of these voters is below their dignity. To this, again, there are exceptions, but the selfish motives of the political class at large are too insistent to ignore.

Another trend I have observed is that our politicians are very poor listeners. They exist in a bubble where they are all-knowing, who stand nothing to gain from engaging in a conversation with a commoner.

The skin of a politician changes color upon election, of course. The humble, well-spoken, well-meaning individual suddenly turns condescending and elusive. They forget that the resources they now have access to is not a private privilege; they are mere custodians of what actually belongs to the public. Throughout our interactions, I have been deeply and repeatedly disappointed by how possessive these public leaders are about public possessions.

The power they wield, a constitutionally sanctioned tool to do well for the public good, is distorted by personal, unprofessional motives. Nepotism thrives as common resources are siphoned off to benefit the cronies and close kin. None of this is surprising. What does continue to surprise me is how entrenched these practices have become: despite common knowledge they continue unabated, with the monetary value of scams only rising exponentially to unbelievable sums.

* * *

During work with young girls at our Youth Resource Centre in Katihar, I met a budding soccer player named Shushma. I was overjoyed to see a teenaged girl speak so passionately about football (as it is usually called in India) and about her experience of being in the girls' football team. It is rare for girls from poverty-ridden, underprivileged backgrounds to have such conviction in any case; it is even rarer to see them pursue a bona fide passion.

Shushma was very articulate, and she had much to say. "Our coach is very good and kind. He arranges kits for us. He is one who has arranged all we have had to play. Our coach often has to work very hard to get us our kits. He asks for kits from the MLA but no one supports us." Shushma was aware of more than just the game. I also learned that the team worked very hard to perfect their game under the guidance of the coach. "We practice every morning at six am. We reach the local ground sharp, on time. I have played at the state level and even outside the state. I enjoy football so much. I just love it."

Awed by Shushma's love for the game, I told her that if she pursues football further and continues doing well in the game she might land a job with the Railways or in another Public Sector Unit under the sports quota. This gave her hope for her future. I for my part was happy to meet her, who was so genuinely determined to pursue a career in sports. I am sure there are many like her in our country, but for most of them, the dream is quelled before it can see the light of day. And for people like Shushma the disturbing question remains whether they will ever they get enough financial, institutional, and emotional support to pursue their calling.

I asked the local MLA if he was keen to support girls like her. His answer was categorically negative. "Sanjay ji, we have sanctioned funds for sports dresses for these girls, but they wear the dresses at home too. They do not maintain sports gear well." Clearly, he sorely lacked the capacity to bring about a measurable difference in the life of these budding sports stars. It is these representatives and lawmakers, in full possession and control of resources, and invariably, unwilling to keep the resources out of reach for the poor and deserving. The same public representatives who cannot be motivated to divert funds and resources for constructive changes, however, inaugurate sports events with great enthusiasm. All this amounts to a disheartening and petty paradox.

We do not always lack resources, we also lack an expansive vision.

I kept turning over Shushma's future in my mind, and kept my eyes open for similar instances of passion among girls in the cities, and the hills. It is rare to see girls participating in the playgrounds and on the streets in India. Yes, a privileged class uses indoor facilities like gyms, swimming pools, private grounds, but among the less privileged, only boys make use of the playground, or the streets.

Where are adolescent girls from poor, underprivileged backgrounds burning their energy? This became a huge question for me and I decided to conduct research on the subject, and author a few opinion pieces to become a vocal rather than silent and passive advocate for female physical activity. Girls in our country are physically inactive compared with boys, especially while growing up. Even if I couldn't force policy makers and local legislators into action, I could do my part to spread awareness.

* * *

During another interaction with a local Member of Parliament from Katihar I proposed the formation of a District Development Plan under his aegis, which would entail strategies to help deal with unemployment, promote of local industry, and improve healthcare and education facilities. I suggested we bring in experts to guide the plan and implement it within a year's time. I also tried to convince the MP to bring on board government officials, NGOs, and donor agencies onto one platform, and then work towards implementing the Development Plan's goals in a time-bound manner. Such a model of execution was sure to bring in positive results.

The MP, unsurprisingly by now, didn't show the least interest. Such politicians hardly invest themselves in bringing about long-term change. Their priority is an immediate, myopic concern with the voter base. It is hard to find leaders who think beyond the five year electoral time frame, and that too in a comprehensive manner. This, in my opinion, is among the strongest factors hindering growth and progress in the country. These policy and law makers, with resources at their disposal, desperately need vision and wisdom to understand what to do with them!

* * *

I was in high school when I stopped using my surname. I didn't want anyone to be aware of my caste. I was only in grade 7, and I took the decision independently, neither consulting anyone, nor seeking approval. It was among the first big decisions I made in life.

I had applied for admission to the Military School that year, and travelled to Patna to appear for the interview. The interviewers noticed the difference in my father's and my surname, and asked about it. I explained the reason as honestly as I could. Of course they were not expecting an opinionated stand in a twelve year old, that too from a caste-sensitive state like Bihar. Here, caste was everything. It determined whether you had any social currency or not. In fact people would be keen to fish for details about your family, your district, your village, and on and on. Your background was everything to the exclusion of your identity or actions; your identity in isolation meant nothing here.

I recognized caste as an insidious evil early, one that had settled in most people's psyches. The 'smart' merely exploited the concept to their advantage. The self-proclaimed caste leaders seldom came forward to further the actual growth and development of their caste-brethren. Rather, they used caste to keep their political and emotional influence alive, and further instead their own, narrow objectives.

Caste loyalties also often demanded that people let go of opportunities for growth. Under pressure to keep caste alliances strong, many lose out on lucrative chances for collaboration. More than anything, caste builds a fractured social ecosystem, where all logic of co-existence and development is defeated through parochial loyalties which demand absolute, blind devotion, as well as a blatant rejection of people from castes not yours. Whether it was my work with Mahadalitsin Katihar, or my interaction with caste leaders in DU and JNU, the presence of caste associations in politics was ubiquitous. They also created small pockets of caste alliances which refused to look beyond at any larger picture of progress – collective or individual. There is of course no recognition of how liberating and empowering it is to interact with people from different socioeconomic backgrounds, how enriching to the self a broader understanding of humanity.

Most of this learning happened outside the classroom. But all these interactions and this exposure grew in me a powerful need to build people with strong character and virtue in our society. I got many opportunities to interact with young college students from different sections of society and I have come to believe we must focus on encouraging them to either participate directly in public services and offices or indirectly engage in public affairs. I found students just out from school and heading to college the most promising. I try to engage with them in whatever social action I design and give them the most active role. With correct guidance and motivation, these young people can do wonders.

Society is a melting pot of people. I intend to bring positive and enthusiastic people together to do some meaningful work on the ground. However, I also intend to learn from those who think more about themselves than about society. My task, I feel, is to take them along the process of change too. In the words of spiritual leader, Shri Shri Anandamurti, "The wisdom of society lies in moving together. If in the course of the journey anybody lags behind, if in the darkness of night a gust of wind blows out anyone's lamp, we shouldn't just go ahead and leave them in lurch. We should extend a hand to help them, and rekindle their lamps with the flames of our lamps."

Chapter Twelve

Another Educational Destination

The urge to learn is of course not the sole prerogative of the young. Harvard was never even on my radar, at least not till forty, when many claim the time to learn is past. In my experience, however, the conscious learning of maturity has had the most immediate and deeply felt impact on my life after.

My background did in one respect serve to limit my aspirations. DU and JNU were the height of ambition; there was barely any concept of going 'abroad'. In the case of students who came from resource scarce places, even imagination has restricted access. Through childhood and early youth I was under the impression only students from extremely privileged backgrounds can leave the country for educational purposes. I only learned that foreign governments, foundations, and universities provide scholarships to support the international academic pursuits of meritorious students from developing countries, especially those involved in public service or in need of funding, much much later.

But then, my decisions and actions through life can hardly be termed precocious. And again, I waited to apply for a program at Harvard long years after I had been regularly writing letters of recommendation for young professionals to facilitate their sojourns to places like the London School of Economics, or Harvard itself.

* * *

After three years with SEWA I had begun exploring the possibility of pursuing a short course or some relevant training abroad. I thought it would be beneficial for both SEWA and myself. I heard about a three-month diploma course on Universalizing Social Security for the Poor, the International Institute of Social Studies in the Hague was piloting, in partnership with SEWA and the Centre for Development Studies, Trivandrum. I applied, and received both admission and a scholarship courtesy the Dutch government.

Though I stayed there for a mere 40 days, the insight I gained to western learning was invaluable. The classrooms, the library, the professors, and the students – everything and everyone had so much to offer. The entire ecosystem sloshed with knowledge like a river in flood rather than the slow drip I had been accustomed to. Professor Ashwani Saith's lectures in Developmental Economics – his scope was tremendous!

I felt I was late getting to a place like the ISS (International Institute of Social Studies). In addition to being an intellectually vibrant academic space, students from multiple cultures and of many nationalities cohabited and co-learned to create a distinct, harmonious culture. I have always surrounded myself with wide varieties of people, from different backgrounds, but this was a first - international diversity. The texture and kind of learning in an explicitly multicultural environment is wholly different from any other. And the Professors were universally competent and approachable.

The Hague too is a truly international city. I explored it in bits and pieces, whenever I could manage to squeeze out time. The visually stunning structure that houses the International Court of Justice, for instance, was only a few blocks away from ISS and of course an everyday delight especially for a student of Political Science.

I also explored other European cities while in the Netherlands, Brussels and Paris, for example, with friends. Paris was awe-inspiring, but I was there alone on my second marriage anniversary…I relieved my feelings by calling Seema from the middle of the Seine.

Of the several good, prosaic civilian practices that struck me forcefully, and I wished to see emulated in Delhi or Katihar, the Dutch Prime Minister's travel to and from the city center via bicycle rather than a cavalcade of disruptive and self-important vehicles that leave snarls of traffic jammed in their wake became symbolic. The Prime Minister of the country went to office on a bicycle. In a class conscious, still feudal society like ours, such a thing could surely never be?

The streets of the Hague were spick and span. I had only, perhaps, seen such neat streets in movies. The cleanliness was supported by good civic sense on the part of citizens, with perhaps one exception – smokers alone throw cigarette butts on the streets.

And for the third I have to thank my brother's friend Ajay Narain, whom I visited in in Amsterdam. Ajay was taking his car out of the parking lot to take me on a trip of the neighborhood, particularly to see the windmills in a nearby village. While reversing, he hit the car parked next to him. He immediately fished a piece of paper out of his pocket, and left a note on the car with his name, number, and apartment address. I was perplexed. Why would someone admit, "Hey, I have slightly damaged your car. Here is my apartment number. Come over at your convenience and let's talk about repair costs." Incredible and weird, but it made so much sense. "Self-declaration helps establish trust among individuals," said Ajay simply, "leading to the creation of a better community," explained Ajay. "The rest is a matter of honest communication, and issues get sorted through long before they become too unwieldy.

While at the Hague, I also became quite a tolerable cook. Restaurant food and takeaways were expensive, so cooking was the only option. I was sharing a kitchen with four others. Joren, a Dutch neighbor of mine, was always super-enthusiastic about cooking. "Cooking is fun, Sanjay," he would say, and gradually I started taking an interest in it too. I became a 'daal expert' and my lentil dishes were in high demand among peers and neighbors. Another perk of living in a multicultural society is the kinds of cuisines you get to sample and enjoy, while familiarizing others to your own culture through its flavors and ingredients. And in this regard India has so much to offer!

* * *

The forty-day trip to the Hague was a great window for me to peep into western education and a western social milieu. It left me desirous of studying more – a hunger I wasn't aware existed of till I ventured out. During this stay, I learned once again mostly by observing people's behavior – how they participated in civic discourse, how passionate they were about learning, how they created common spaces and then each took on the onus of maintaining it. It was also heartening to see how inclusive the city was, welcoming and accepting students who came from all over the world. Back home in India, students and professionals migrating from smaller towns and villages are often treated as pariahs, not finding acceptance and inclusion till long after they have assimilated. This limitation of kinship is a cruel hindrance to national progress.

* * *

After coming back from ISS, I noticed that people with even one foreign degree in their belt occupied top positions in different sectors. In addition, they do things differently, their practices drawn from exposure and experiences abroad. They are more open in their outlook, their horizons broadened due to high quality education. This further cemented the advantage of foreign education in my mind.

Around 2005-06, I was beginning to realize that individuals who'd studied abroad did thing differently: their practices were more systematic, open, and tolerant of feedback and change: their horizons are broadened by the experience. I realized too that they came to invariably occupy top positions in various sectors… I began thinking of my Ph.D. again, which had been on hold for a long time, owing to my professional commitments. I had taken a break from my Ph.D. work under a generous provision at JNU, but now wrote it up: *Microfinance interventions among Poor Women: A comparative Case Study of SEWA Bank in India and BRAC in Bangladesh* was submitted in 2008 and I was awarded with my doctoral degree in 2009.

* * *

Three important life events – the Hands of Hope photo project, the PG Diploma from ISS and my Ph.D. from JNU – made me aspire for still more in education. My work, of course, continued with the same enthusiasm.

Like many individuals, I also hit a mid-career crisis. Confusion and chaos regarding future options muddled my brain. In early 2010, I often caught myself involuntarily questioning my choice of career. Should I switch to another organization? Should I look for a new career altogether? These were questions that suddenly loomed large.

Many new thoughts enticed me. I thought of switching over from my current stream of work to journalism or academia. At the same time, I wanted to nourish the activist in myself further. Introspection and deep-thinking is imperative for personal growth, but it can also leave you vulnerable. Along with the excitement of exploring new terrains, thinking can cripple you with nervousness as you consciously exit your comfort zones. I could exit my current professional role and join another organization for a short time, but what good would a year or two in a new job do me? Finally, it was settled that I would take a sabbatical from work to pursue studies and satisfy the craving assailing me for some time.

* * *

Taking a sabbatical wasn't an easy decision. It meant I would take a year off from SEWA. It meant convincing many people and seeking official permissions. No one within the organization had taken such a long hiatus from work. This was the first challenge. The second was formulating a plan to ensure my family could accompany me. And the third and biggest challenge was money. I simply didn't have any!

* * *

In early 2012, the idea had been thought through, discussed and validated. SEWA chairperson Renanaben agreed; Seema only bolstered the idea that this must be an opportunity for the entire family to acquire exposure. I now began searching for course options. There was only one that appealed, and resonated with my broader aims. The Master's in Public Administration for mid-career aspirants at the Harvard Kennedy School had to be my next education destination. Period.

* * *

The goal was set, path yet to be ascertained. How to get to Harvard?

I was broadly familiar with the detailed application process universities like Harvard demanded. I now had to find out more about funding, come up with a plan for supporting my wife and kids, budgeting family expenses, and finding people who could write recommendations for me. My application needed to be strong.

Essay writing was strenuous. It took me about a week just to conceptualize the essays and decide on what and how I wanted to write. I had to pick and choose experiences to cite since there was a word limit. I discovered that the need to be crisp and appealing at once helped get in deeper touch with my own thought processes. Experiential learning was reiterated. While figuring my way through words, I also remained confident; what I was expressing was personal to me. These essays were genuine expressions of the deepest hopes I had, which I wanted to convert into action to serve communities across India. I was also mindful of remaining wholly myself - the only originality genuinely possible.

Through the application process I was fortunate too to have a mentor of sorts. Mr. Rohit Kumar Singh was Project Director for a community infrastructure program we had undertaken in Bikaner, Rajasthan. He too had done the same course a few years earlier. A dynamic and dedicated professional, he had been very encouraging during our meeting in Jaipur. He guided me through to the completion of application process in time. His inputs were also useful for taking the family with me.

* * *

The waiting period between submission and declaration of results wasn't too long, but it did leave me impatient, panicky, nervous and in a strange thrilled state. Since I had been vocal about my intent to go to Harvard, everyone kept asking after the result, heightening my already great nervousness.

By the time the date of results approached my desperation had reached its peak. I had begun discussing back-up plans. But I was also already visualizing days in Cambridge – how I would be a student again, how my son and daughter would attend a local school, how the whole family would spend quality time together and explore the beautiful places around Cambridge, and most of all, how I would get this superlative chance to completely immerse myself in learning concepts I could later apply. In short, Harvard was not just a dream, it had become *the* dream.

I was in Jaipur with my family when I woke up with a jerk at 5 am one morning. Instantly, like propelled by an outward force, I headed to check my email. Still groggy, I opened the laptop, logged in and there it was – my admission offer letter from the Dean of the Kennedy School, along with a welcome video.

I have, to date, not figured out an apt set of words to express how I felt in that moment. Jovial. Elated. On cloud nine. On top of the world. Amazed. Relieved. Add a million more words here and I still couldn't enunciate the emotions that coursed through me.

In the midst of all this rush of feelings, I went through the mail and the video. A part of me, the skeptical one, wanted to confirm and reconfirm if there was any mistake. Great excitement is accompanied with a strange mix of disbelief, and I wanted to be sure that I had understood the mail correctly, and that my comprehension was not marred by the half-sleepy state I was still in.

It was, indeed a mail confirming my admission. While there was no news of scholarship as yet, I was still thrilled. My brain returning to normalcy, I felt the acute need to share this super news with someone. I woke Seema up and as her mind registered what was happening, I saw a smile alight on her face and in no time, she was aglow with joy as great as my own. She was calmer than me, but I knew she was equally thrilled.

I then called up my mother and brother, and after seeking their blessing, the series of phone calls continued to people who had been with me in the application process. Seema and I then woke the kids up. Chaitanya displayed uncontained excitement upon hearing the news. Tathya hardly understood anything, but the joyous atmosphere made her giggle and smile too. All she could comprehend was that we would all be going somewhere together, for a long time!

* * *

When the excitement subsided began to process that there was no news on scholarship. If this didn't come through, Harvard would remain a dream.

The chagrin didn't last long, since the very next mail I received was one with a link to the Harvard Scholarship portal. Excited and tense, I opened the link and my jaw dropped. I had been awarded a scholarship of 90,926 USD! I was not able to read anything written around this figure. There were words and statements, but my eyes remained focused on the numeric amount. This was enough to cover fees, living expenses, and even the application fee of 750 USD, which had been returned with this amount. I was in tears. Literally.

From the day I had been designated a failure, to the words on my scholarship letter, praising my "commitment to the principles of democratic governance and public service" and "capacity to innovate and implement non-traditional approaches to social and economic development" I had travelled an incredible distance. It seemed unreal, all of it. More so when I contrasted my achievement of the day with the ruins of the past. I had made it! Against all odds, against resource scarcity, against words of discouragement, against my own sense of diffidence, I had arrived at a juncture where my faith in my own abilities ought to be complete and the world was echoing confidence.

❑❑

Chapter Thirteen

Life at Harvard

If I had to find an apt expression for the phase that built up to life at Harvard, I would describe it as excited chaos. Everyone at home was involved, excited and busy preparing for the departure. Passports and visas had been applied for. Shopping was under way. Chaitanya was ten or twelve, and he had many questions to ask, the answers to which only served to heighten his excitement for the impending trip. Tathya was only four, so she couldn't comprehend much till the day we actually landed in Boston. Seema was happy to too, but her happiness drew from the fact that all of us were going to be together.

On the early evening of 23rd June we landed in Boston. The curious eyes of my family were looking around, soaking in and admiring this new world. Their faces were aglow with the thrill of a new kind of life in a land far, far away from our own. While enjoying the rush of emotions with my family, I also kept reminding myself that I was here for a deep dive into academia; we hailed a cab to Peabody Terrace, a Harvard Housing Apartment complex.

* * *

We reached Peabody Terrace around 8 pm. This was going to be our home for the next year. The house was completely bare, with nothing in it. We had lugged along our clothes and essentials, but weren't sure how we would furnish this beautiful but naked space. These questions, however, could be answered later. Right then we were hungry. Venturing out to eat after such a long journey was unanimously dismissed and our homemade 'sattu paranthas' came to the rescue. A Bihari staple, they had been lovingly packed for us by my younger sister, Sangita.

The next morning, excitement woke us all rather early. My children peeped through the back door and enthusiastically called out to me. When I followed the exhilaration in their voices, I realized there was a children's park right behind our apartment. Our accommodation had a special gate which directly opened into it. No wonder my kids were shrieking with joy. In the days to come, Chaitanya and Tathya were often spotted hopping and prancing about the park; it became an extension of our house. My kids, albeit for a short time, but were going to be nurtured in an environment which was safe, secure, stimulating, clean, encouraging, nourishing – in short, they would be exposed to the quality of life which I had had no access to for the greater part of my life.

As the kids went ahead with their exploration, Seema and I busied ourselves setting the house in order. The first space we set up was the kitchen. Seema was determined that we were not going to waste any money towards eating out. Since the very first day she ensured we got the comfort of home cooked food even in this alien land. The basic utensils and ingredients we had carried along came to be of much use.

Furniture followed, and our collective gasps of delight soon normalized into the hum of routine. 30th June was a significant date – this is when my classes started. As on any new journey, trepidation accompanied thrill. This was not a normal new, but it was a very old new. I was going back to the classroom after 15 years! I was unsure about how the space would feel this time, but great learning was in store, that I was sure about.

The faculty at the Kennedy School made us comfortable with their welcome speeches. I was also looking forward to the wonderful opportunity of interacting with people from such a wide range of nationalities. In the first two weeks, 90 students from 55 developing countries joined in summer classes. Within some time, we became a cohort of 217 students in one class, from 75 different countries. The diversity was mind-boggling!

Classes were scheduled from nine am to six pm. The schedule was sapping, but rewarding too. Most mornings I felt excited to ready myself for 'school'. I couldn't help but smile at myself; till a few days ago I was readying my kids for school, and now it was me looking forward to lectures, to homework, researching for assignments, and generally excited to don the proverbial uniform.

Like any student, I had my fears too. Foremost among these was Math. This scary subject had re-entered my life after twenty five years but the usual dread was expertly contained by our Romanian math teacher, Stas Marian. He was a very diligent, committed instructor, who took us back to the most fundamental concepts. In a matter of two weeks, he succeeded in making the entire batch friendly with the subject. One could see that this man was an expert not just in his subject, but at understanding the diverse contexts and psyches of his students, most of whom had not touched Math for decades. His empathy made Stas a great teacher.

The Mason Program starts early July, long before the regular schools. Consequently the campus was mostly bare but for the ninety of us Mason Fellows ambling here and there. The atmosphere was serene. By the time our number expanded to two hundred seventeen, we had all settled into our classes, lifestyle, and social groups. The composition of the class was awesome, diverse not just in terms of nationalities, but every other parameter of identity. We had classmates with backgrounds in the navy, in politics, in journalism, in law, in government, civil society movements, consulting, and many other niche fields which I was learning about for the first time. This program attracts the best globally – people who are engaged in pathbreaking, innovative work in their respective fields.

I enjoyed learning about and from each of them, hearing their stories, everyday.

* * *

Before the academic session began full swing in September, we got a two-week break. This was our time to settle down, explore Boston and nearby areas, and most importantly, to get to know our classmates better. These social calls became even more fun and exciting when potluck became popular. Food binds like nothing else. At these potluck parties, we would all carry delicacies from our part of the world and conversations would flow on all aspects of culture, driven by but not limited to food. That these sessions were a family affair for me and for others added to their warmth.

The Indian food we took along was especially popular. Curry was a favorite with everyone and we had a variety to offer. Dinners at our place too became frequent, both for the students and for faculty. The love which food and flavors generated was heartening.

Come September, when the number of students on campus suddenly spiked, our lives became crowded, but also livelier! A natural vibrancy settled in to the weave of days and so many cultures, languages, and sensibilities passed in and out of them.

One day, we heard a curious thing. A samosa-chaat party was being organized by the South Asia Institute on campus. In the two months since we had arrived on the campus, we had not even heard mention of chaat, let alone feast on them. With childlike enthusiasm we reached the venue with our other South Asian friends. It is amazing what the smell of familiar food can do to you. Olfactory associations bring back the strongest memories, along with the overpowering sense of nostalgia. Chaat-Samosa-and-Chai, that's all it took to take us back to the streets of India and instantly bond with fellow South Asians over the shared nostalgia.

It was at this party that I was introduced to Professor Tarun Khanna of the Harvard Business School, who was heading the Harvard South Asia Institute. He was later instrumental in opening the institute's India office in Delhi, and I became its first Country Director.

* * *

We had to choose our classes for the fall semester. Making this choice was slightly stressful, since the better teachers and their courses were always in high demand. We were given 1000 'points' to 'shop' for our favorite courses. We had to shop for these courses basis information provided by an online portal, where the objective, scope, readings and evaluation scheme for the course were listed, and through talk sessions with the faculty members who were going to deliver it. The process itself was exhilarating, especially since I managed to bag most of my preferred courses.

Come September, classes took off full swing. Being inside the classrooms often evoked memories of my time at the International Institute of Social Studies, which had inspired me to take up study again in the first place. The degree of expertise and professionalism displayed by faculty at Harvard was of the highest standard. Our mentors led by example. The hard work and pedagogical meticulousness that went into each class was discernible. They respected time, minded their own attendance and conduct, and made sure they had done their own homework - were adequately prepared to take the lecture. They gave students a chance to speak up and generally encouraged a culture of questioning and inquiry. Classrooms discussions with such professors were empowering, liberating, and expanded our minds. Each class was different, each learning experience was unique. We owed our professors credit for creating such a wholesome environment for study.

In many of our classes we were studying alongside our peers from different programs. This enabled a further diverse interface; and this time also in terms of age. The dynamics of discussion in an age-diverse group were very interesting to observe. The mid-career students unconsciously displayed a sense of superiority with respect to knowledge and experience. The youngsters remained belligerent and defensive while trying to convince the cohort to their fresh points of view and perspectives. Coming to cohesive conclusions in such situations was difficult, since everyone was toeing a different line. Once we realized and accepted how significant a role ageism was playing in our conversations, it became a lot easier to enjoy these discussions.

* * *

We were allowed to choose two classes outside the Kennedy School during the academic year. I was keen to do a course at the Harvard

Business School. Having worked extensively in the development field, I hoped that knowledge of business strategy would aid in the modeling and scaling up of social enterprises owned by the poor. I was not able to find the exact class I was looking for, so I settled for a course called 'Business at the Base of the Pyramid'. It sounded like something which could benefit my field of engagement.

Upon closer inspection, I realized that this course focused more on understanding the poor as a 'market'. This definitely seemed like an opportunity to gain fresh insight, with excellent faculty and dynamic classes. Most of the students here were doing their MBA from HBS. The batch taking this course, consisting of about ninety students, was extremely bright, vocal, and well-informed.

Before each class we were provided with a case study, which we would discuss in detail in the classroom. The methodology and approach was superb. The professors would also give a cold call (make a surprise call to any student in the classroom) to ensure everyone remained serious. We as students were also expected to present case studies and information relevant to the course to the class. I was once asked to talk about Grameen Danone Foods to open the class and since I had read the case thoroughly, I was able to do so. Sure, it was pretty scary, but after my initial opening monologue, the entire class came together to discuss, debate, and participate in a holistic dialogue.

The HBS students were subjects of a peculiar kind of prejudice. One commonly heard that they were arrogant, rude, and only interested in learning about business. Well, they were. But studying alongside them, I also realized they were all super-bright and perhaps, intimidating to their peers. Once you had an open conversation with them, you realized how 'normal' they were outside the bubble of prejudgment. I made some great friends among the HBS students. Karan Kapoor was one such. We sat together in class and carried on discussions of our own that continued long past normal school hours.

* * *

This is not to say that the campus was free of intellectual arrogance. I had witnessed it back home in universities in Delhi, and I was sure I would meet my fair share in Harvard. Some students carried their sense of exclusivity and superiority into behavior with fellow-students as well. They seemed to be chasing a version of themselves as elite and classy, and this desire manifested in ugly behavior that deemed all others lesser human beings. I was not the only one who sensed this. When I opened up about this with other classmates, I realized others had been observing and noting this too.

The importance of humility cannot be overstated, especially in learning environments where so many cultures intermingle. Observing arrogance in others reinforced this thought for me and made me commit further to staying grounded.

Harvard is Harvard because of the people who inhabit it – the faculty, staff, scholars and students. They comprise the coveted Harvard ecosystem, which is an great intellectual stimulant and among the top places in the world for a holistic teaching-learning exercise. Knowledge at Harvard doesn't stagnate; it results from a dynamic interaction between thought, research, world affairs and discourse/discussion.

A certain degree of dynamism is also lent to the Harvard ecosystem due to the presence of vast diversity of people from all corners of the world. New thoughts, hence, are always getting infused into the stream of intellectual discourse. It is an eclectic and exciting place to be in.

Yet Harvard does suffer pitfalls of its own, however invisible they may sometimes be. I had imagined that students of all backgrounds and geographies would be equal at Harvard, but intellectual arrogance had succeeded in finding quite a few victims amongst us. Groups of common ethnicities had formed among students, and they refused to acknowledge others they considered inferior. Yes, 'othering' was a phenomenon in this University.

Harvard has an elitist reputation, and this kind of student behavior only cemented it. The experienced I had while dealing with some of my American classmates were echoed by fellow students from developing nations. If students cannot open their mind and act in humility even after reaching the highest citadel of education, what good is any learning?

This is not to say that all, or even many, experiences were bad. I had several American classmates who were cheerful, unassuming and friendly. It was they who made our time worthwhile on the campus.

And while I am in a critiquing frame, it must be said that Harvard, and other similar institutes, are prohibitively expensive (bar limited scholarship opportunities). Harvard's own housing is exorbitant, compared to nearby areas. As a result, for most of the aspirants, Harvard only remains a far-fetched dream unless they rank among the handful few who have been able to bag scholarships. Even then, they have to house themselves far away from the campus, for the lack of reasonably priced accommodation on campus. I do believe, as a result of this, some genuine talent is not able to reach the hallowed gates of the University. This world class education should be available to yet more people.

* * *

The Winter term, or the 'J Term' as it was popularly known, is an altogether different experience. It was one of the harshest winters in Boston, but students managed to have a blast even during blizzards. Many, including Seema, were seeing snow for the first time. They were determined to enjoy this new experience to the fullest! Making Snowmen was a favorite activity, unveiling the child hidden among all these adults. Charles River near our home was frozen and people took great pleasure walking on it.

The Bostoners' love for jogging was incorrigible. Even in extreme climates, you could see them running and walking. And Christmas celebrations at the Boston Commons were of course majestic. Bright, beautiful, lit-up, and warm – the thrill was too great to express precisely in words. We went through an entire cycle of seasons in Boston, but the winters were undoubtedly the most fun!

The Harvard Campus service was very prompt in clearing snow off the campus, making stay inside very convenient. Those of our classmates who stayed in accommodations of their own did share how difficult it was to clear all the snow lining their driveways and homes on their own. They couldn't afford to hire help for this, since labor is expensive in Boston.

* * *

The winter classes were an intensive affair that lasted two weeks. I had chosen a class on Leadership taken by Professor Ronald Heifetz during this semester. He was one of the best and most popular professors at Harvard. Students used to bid their entire 1000 points to get into his class. During the J Term, he had about 110 students. Other than his personality and subject expertise, his pedagogical technique was exceptional. While clearly remaining at the center of the class, he used to orchestrate the lesson plans in such a way that he would speak less and encourage students to speak up and discuss more. He would pitch in only when he thought necessary, decisively and with clarity, bringing the class discussion toward a comprehensive conclusion.

His concept of leadership was not to lead from the front, but to work together with and in a group. According to him, leaders should understand the dynamics of those they are working with, have a finger on the pulse of emotions and opinions among them, and then adapt in order to bring about changes and implement work effectively. This theory can be applied at work, in community service, and even in family situations.

His main theory is known as 'Adaptive Leadership' theory. The way we learnt about it was through case presentations, long discussions, focused discussions in smaller groups, all enriched with his valuable insights and comments. Holding together and streamlining a discussion in a class of 110 was challenging, especially on topics which were controversial or naturally complicated. But he was in control without dominating. He was inspiring as well as approachable. I think among all the teachers I have had the privilege of learning from in life, Professor Heifetz has been the most impactful.

* * *

I took classes at the Kennedy School, the Business School, and the Design School at Harvard. American universities have a common library system, where you can place a request for any book if it is available in participating universities, even across cities and states.

Seminars and discussions are routinely organized around Harvard, and celebrated figures from different fields invited to campus for an engagement session or a guest lecture.

Harvard has of course great convening power. The Kennedy School forum is one of the most sought after venues for hosting talks and discussions. I got to meet a lot of prominent people, including Indian ministers, both currently serving and former, well-known academics, and civil practitioners.

Among the most significant interactions was one with Noam Chomsky. He lives in Boston. To meet a luminary thinker and academic like him was of course a great privilege and our peer group was aflutter with excitement. During the question-answer session, one of my classmates asked him, "Sir, you write extensively against the United States of America, especially its dictatorial foreign policy. Do you not feel threatened living in a country which you so openly criticize?"

Mr. Chomsky's answer was very interesting, "No. I never feel threatened in this country because this is the only country which truly believes in your democratic rights. However you may criticize the establishment and its policies, you are never touched." Of course, I started visualizing the same statement in the Indian context: where do we stand as a democracy when it comes to contrary opinions and challenging the establishing? Are we, as a nation, tolerant enough to hear perspectives uncomfortably different from our own? How many journalists, activists, civil servants, and others are killed, lose their jobs, or are otherwise harassed for dissent, every year?

It must be acknowledged that, without exception, differing perspectives were respected at Harvard in all discussions I was part of. Discussions in the classroom often got heated, but even then, people would give others space for expressing contrary opinions. We would listen to each other and give our fellow speakers the respect they deserved for sharing their view-point. We wouldn't jump in till a statement was completed. We might not agree with a statement, but that did not mean we turned against the person. We were a diverse set, brought up in different cultures, of different backgrounds, and values. This diversity also caused differences of opinions and arguments, but we understood and respected this.

Often, I also realized how weak and even irrelevant my stands were on certain topics were. This happened only through an openness to hear and understand what the other was saying. The kind of learning I craved required an ecosystem which encouraged and supported diversity, not just in terms of people, but also in terms of thought. Harvard was the perfect place for that.

* * *

Apart from key analytical skills and subject knowledge, the key thing at a place like Harvard is people – who they are, how they present themselves, what drives them. What I witnessed here was very different from India. There was a general belief and trust in self-declaration. People would trust your words. Such an environment, I found, did not encourage deceit or tale-telling or misrepresentation; it encouraged truth, and introspection.

Being a part of the Harvard community was fun. So much was always happening around us, and an empowered student community was at the center of organizing most of it. I too decided to run for the position of Kennedy School Student Union President. Much deliberation and convincing ensued – lobbying and persuasion are an important part of any political theatre. Finally my sole opponent's popularity and energy convinced me that he was a better candidate. I couldn't win against him, but we did end up being good friends.

* * *

I was also part of the Organizing Team for the Indian Conference at Harvard. Sagar Preet Hooda, a classmate and a very good friend of mine, and I took the lead to organize a keynote panel on women's empowerment. Women's issues were usually debated on ordinary panels, but this time we decided to put them right under the spotlight. Our list of speakers included Kiran Bedi, Renena Jhabvala from SEWA, and for his popularity, Bollywood actor Rahul Bose. The panel was moderated by Martha Chen from the Kennedy School, and a huge success. The three of them brought different perspectives to the discussion and the current challenges the country was facing in terms of safety and security of women, particularly post-Nirbhaya.

I also took the initiative starting an 'India Matters' discussion series at Kennedy School, which took place every Friday. It was organized under the India Caucus. We were responsible for bringing eminent intellectuals and professionals to discuss key issues pertaining to India. We were able to host the then Environment Minister Prakash Javdekar, ex-Environment and Rural Development Minister. Jairam Ramesh, scholars such as Professor Jacqueline Bhabha, Professor Bishwapriya Sanyal and Dr Kulwinder Kaur, and others.

The Kennedy School organized its Annual Talent Show at year's end. I had nothing to showcase, but Chaitanya had been learning Western Vocals from a Harvard student under the community engagement program. The opportunity to perform on the Harvard stage got him excited, and he agreed to perform *Lay Me Down* by Sam Smith in front of a stunned audience including the Dean of Kennedy School, who gave him a standing ovation.

Tathya, too, grew in confidence through her pre-school experience at Harvard and engagement with kids there. Once when she and Chaitanya were fighting, she told him to please go away and leave her alone. "I need my space." Born to a background where women weren't supposed to have a voice at all, I was touched and thrilled to see my daughter growing up with positive values, and being assertive. What she had learned at five, I was sure, was going to go a long way in shaping Tathya into a smart, confident, strong woman.

Seema too had a good time at Harvard. She and I divided chores, but she derived much pleasure from supporting all of us in every manner possible. She also audited two classes – one at Harvard School of Public Health and another at the Kennedy School. She made most of her time there, and was veritably the glue holding us together. The treasure of pictures and videos she collected through our year at Harvard is the most cherished souvenir we have carried back.

* * *

Time at Harvard flew past. At the Convocation I was assailed by a strange and disturbing feeling of disbelief - but I earned my

Harvard degree. I missed my father intensely, and rued the fact that he couldn't witness that moment. He was the man who rode bicycles across Katihar so our educational expenses could be taken care of the man who couldn't complete his education because family conditions didn't permit him to do so. He had never heard of a university outside India and his son was getting a degree from Harvard!

I had promised him that I would never give up my study. I was glad I had kept and fulfilled that promise.

* * *

My Harvard journey did not end with the degree. It was the beginning of many new things to come. My mind, which had undergone tremendous expansion through the past year, was determined to do more and more and more. With a lot of energy and new perspectives we left Boston at the end of July, a little more than a year after we arrived. For everyone in our family this was a year of individual and collective learning, grown wisdom and knowledge that may have been hard to gather in a much greater time span, had we remained still. This was the gift of the Harvard ecosystem. Everyone took a leap thereafter.

❑❑

Chapter Fourteen

Life after Harvard

Our Convocation took place in May. In early June, I found a quiet moment to sip tea by the Charles River. In the gushing current of the river, I found the gushing flow of my life – not just this past year at Harvard, but everything, on from childhood. Family, work, friends from India – everything hit me with an unwonted nostalgia. I was glad I was going back soon.

'Yeh jo des hai tera' - the song actually started playing in my head. I was involuntarily humming along. This one song by A. R. Rehman, I've found, invariably overwhelms Indians abroad, and motivates them to action for their country… I finished my tea lost in the same reverie. Back home I asked Chaitanya if he would like to see *Swades* with me. The whole family got together to watch the Ashutosh Gowarikar film. The movie too evoked intense emotion, and reminded me of all the tasks and responsibilities back home.

Yes. It was time to come back and pick up work again. It was time to start drafting another chapter in life.

Narendra, who hails from Katihar but is now an American citizen, came to see us off with his family on our last day in Cambridge. We had known each other in childhood - though two years my senior I had always found him affable, easy to get along with, cheerful and energetic wherever he went, and in any circumstances - but we hadn't remained in touch. Our reconnection happened when my article was published by NDTV. Facebook was instrumental in bringing us back together. Once he located me there, we never lost touch. In fact, we met quite a few times to relive stories of Katihar and deliberate on issues we both felt deeply about. It was an unbelievable coincidence to meet someone from Katihar in Boston. The connections of our land run deep. Narendra stayed with us a whole day before we left, departing just before the time we set out towards the Airport.

* * *

We got back to Delhi on the morning of 29th July, 2015. It was still dark outside when we set foot in the house. It took only a few seconds for Seema and I to realize there was a power cut and the battery-run inverter too had malfunctioned, after all this time. The house was plunged in blinding darkness. Tathya got really scared – in her young mind, this was a new phenomenon. She hadn't witnessed any power cuts in Boston, and a year is a long time for the very young. She was so frightened she clung to us.

We took her shopping the next day. As soon as we got onto the main road, Tathya yelled, "Papa! Why is there so much noise? Why are people honking so much!" Poor child. She had forgotten her time in Delhi, and was experiencing what they call 'reverse culture shock'.

Chaitanya too went through a hard time, especially in school. Both he and his sister had adapted to the liberal American education system, with relatively small class sizes. Our Indian education system is closed and rigorous, which my children had real trouble settling into. It was only when they were admitted to a private school with a progressive, constructivist pedagogical approach that they regained their enthusiasm and started looking forward to being in the school everyday.

Settling down took a while for Seema too. She had decided to venture into something new - an arts-based enterprise. She had worked with several Madhubani artists as a journalist and a documentary film-maker. She wanted to continue film-making, but also started an enterprise with the Madhubani art form at its centre.

Seema's passion for the art form runs deep. She herself learnt Madhubani and received recognition as an artist with the Ministry of Handicrafts. Since then she has been developing an artisan network through her enterprise and building her profile as artist and entrepreneur. She showcased Madhubani wall paintings and clothes at The Bhawan Art Gallery in London.

* * *

I too needed to adapt. The Harvard degree came with baggage - expectations. A branded degree always does excite curiosity of a particular kind: even my insignificant or routine actions, behavior, performance, began to be associated with it. Everything I did, I began to think through with greater care than ever, even second-guess.

Nevertheless, the year at Harvard had indeed added several new dimensions to my personality. I understood biases better and was able to listen to contrary perspectives without getting worked up. I felt armed (and armored) with knowledge and new insight I wanted to put it all to practical use. But where to begin? What grand challenge to take up? I was driven to identify key issues and develop a strategic plan to address them, and to refine my purpose in life. I wanted to find a suitable medium again.

SEWA was always a medium, never an end in itself. I wanted to work for the socioeconomic empowerment of the most disadvantaged strata in our country, and SEWA was the most apposite platform from which to realize this goal. While working with SEWA I had several opportunities to serve marginalized communities, and to create ecosystems of social, economic, and gender justice. I gave it my all. But long before Harvard happened I had realized that I needed to expand my own horizons to serve this cause more effectively. I needed to get acquainted with more than SEWA; any organization is ultimately limited to its adopted scope, purview, people, and methodologies. I needed to break from this familiar space and reaffirm my own, individual vision and mission rather than continuing to operate in accordance with SEWA's. For this, it was necessary that I step back from active involvement with them. People stop aspiring because they get complacent. They think their past achievements are enough, or they think a group or organisation they identify with has done 'enough' good. A student who succeeds in becoming a civil servant and thinks she or he needn't aspire to serve the greater good because being a civil servant is enough - or a social sector worker who thinks she or he needn't develop her or himself or initiate projects because their NGO is doing 'enough' - both I feel are wrong.

* * *

I started meeting people in a deliberate, strategizing manner, from different walks of life. I wanted to understand what kind of work people were doing, what gaps they were filling and where I fit into the picture. I met activists and politicians, academics and bureaucrats, entrepreneurs and lawyers, and many, many young students. I learned that it was true - I was already aware of the problems most of them were in various ways preoccupied with, only now I heard different interpretations or expressions of those problems - different perspectives on causes and what innovative solutions might look like. Everyone was eager to assign blame – some blamed the government, others 'society' as an amorphous abstraction. No one took responsibility to bring about change – I hardly encountered ownership of problems, or collectivization of effort to have real and lasting impact. I found myself beginning to repeat myself in these conversations: we do not need to wait for an NGO to show up and start solving problems. We do not even need to fight the lumbering state machinery for changes in policy and institutional structures before we can act on the ground. We need to create our own initiatives, without dependence on government or other entities, among communities, neighbors, colleagues, friends. Once we achieve this, institutional and state support will organically manifest. And when advocacy is necessary, it is far more effective if tangible results of experiments can be brought to bear on one's arguments.

I also found myself returning time and again to one area of concern: the decline in the quality of public education in India felt like the most breathtakingly tragic waste of all, and a personal affront. I desperately wanted to do something about it. We as a people do have access to advanced technology, to a fairly solid infrastructure of communication, and of course, of human potential, yet the government education system is failing, struggling to survive in most all the country. The problem is compounded by the cascade of mushrooming private educational institutions that are prohibitively expensive for most Indians, that charge exorbitant fees for education that is barely worth the name.

Will private schools and universities inevitably take over the education system in our country the way private hospitals have taken over the public health system? How will the majority of Indians, who survive on less than the bare minimum, be able to afford these institutions? Will not such a system as inevitably deepen socioeconomic divides? How will the state of government institutions improve if public servants and the professional class continue sending their children to private schools and colleges?

I decided to visit Katihar for a reality check before deciding on my course of action.

I began my on-the-ground research by visiting Maheshwari Academy, lauded as one of the best high schools through my childhood. I really was very upset not to have been able to attend school here, then. Now, it is lost. In my time, it was a well-maintained two-storey building within a sprawling campus. Today, the site is ugly from neglect. How can fresh ideas or even bare learning thrive in such a dilapidated place? The terrible, typical irony? The office of the District Education Officer was located on campus. The ruin of education was being played out literally in sight of the DEO.

During that trip I met so many college students who admitted to skipping because their lecturers were seldom on time and rarely interested in taking classes. They'd rather spend their time in private coaching and prepare for competitive exams. Some of their college teachers ran private tuition sessions, which they attended. Simultaneously, these college students enrolled in professional courses to do with computers, design, etc. to augment their CV and make it easier for them to find a job once they graduated. The whole situation was absurd beyond belief, and certainly not geared toward the interest of the students. Colleges should be vibrant spaces where the holistic and individual development of minds and bodies of young people is encouraged, not mere physical spaces for enrolment, a few rare lectures, and examinations.

The situation needs critical attention, and cursing the government is not going to solve anything. In this moment, at least, we need to transcend legislative authority as a matter of urgency and intellectual survival. "Ask not what your country can do for you," said John F. Kennedy, banners across the Kennedy School campus remind its attendees, "but what you can do for your country." If we want to see change in our lifetimes, and leave a still living legacy of knowledge production and dissemination for generations to come, we need to take these words to heart.

I went to visit my high school. The last time I visited I was soon leaving for Harvard. As I set foot on campus I experienced a complex mix of extremely powerful emotions. I felt them again, and more, now. I was probably the first one from this district to earn degrees such as I now had to my name. Despite my anguish and anxiety, my heart brimmed with excitement for the grand door of prospects that had opened up before me. On the other hand, my heart sank for the lack of opportunities this town, its school, and its children will continue to wallow in.

After interacting with the students, I found a quiet moment for myself and sat down on the lone rickety bench in the precincts. A strange ennui descended upon me. Looking around, I felt a storm of questions engulf me. What is the future of the children of this school? What is the future of the people of my town? Is it right for me to look out for myself rather than serving them, somehow? What should I do to give back? Or should I stop bothering altogether? Should I be unconcerned with socioeconomic disparities? Should I shut my eyes to the oppression of and discrimination against women?

It must have been over an hour of silent mulling. The questions coursed through my blood in a truly physical sense. Through the purgatory of pained, chaotic, restless reflection, only one answer seemed to lend some light, on an admittedly distant horizon – education.

I am a product of education - or rather a product of my father's belief in the fruits of education. With every passing moment my belief in the transformative power of education has only grown stronger. If I could travel as far as I have, perched on the wings of its pursuit, so could millions of students across the country. Provided they are not disillusioned, halted in their tracks, or diverted to other occupations and responsibilities. A natural flair, talent, and curiosity exists in each child – it is the purpose of education to carefully nurture these and lead individuals to self-actualization.

I owe my parents a huge moral debt, truly, especially in view of the thousands of young students across the country who struggle in educational and social systems that arrest their growth because no one can envision for them a future, and their own visions are stunted through cruel neglect. To honor them, if nothing else (and there is much else), I was going to remain invested in education, by and alongside working to empower women, through other developmental work. I knew what my purpose and obligation must be, over the next few years.

* * *

I had to diversify my civil society engagement opportunities. It was convenient to continue at SEWA Bharat, but real growth cannot happen without pushing oneself out of the comfort zones one has gotten used to. Coincidentally, and in perfect time, I was offered a position at Harvard – to lead the India office of their South Asia Institute. They were opening a new office in Delhi and wanted me to lead their initiatives across the country.

I was grateful for the recognition, and also felt I would have an excellent framework, facilities, and resources to better understand pedagogy and the logistics involved in delivering quality education. The job would also be a great platform to connect learned knowledge with practical action. Action and social impact programs were already my forte; the chance to work at a prestigious educational research center was a gift, one I could use to design programs with more efficacy and insight, and launch them farther and wider to the benefit of all concerned.

I can say very little about the reality of leaving SEWA. It felt like my organization; I had been emotionally as well as professionally bound up in its people and its work for nearly two decades. Emotions ran thick for several months. We wept, my colleagues were shocked, expressed disapproval and disbelief, expressed despair and asked me to stay on. I changed my mind time and time again, swept up in memory and by the bare fact of the work I could still do. But my original decision had not been lightly made, and was final, really. I remain excruciatingly grateful to the people I have worked with year after year - but move on I must, or stagnate. In this moment what I needed was not an organization designed to deliver specific, if vital, services to individuals in exigent circumstances through an established network, and channels grooved in over decades; I needed to apply what I had learned to build a new kind of delivery system, capable of reaching people before their circumstances deteriorated to the point they could for the most part only hope to flourish vicariously, through the next generation.

I continued writing op-eds on miscellaneous of social and human importance - related to education and to gender disparity. It has become a way of reaching out to people, trying to help develop and influence public opinion on issues that matter. I also continued working on this book, to collate and consolidate my thoughts and my experiences, which I am especially desirous of communicating to students struggling under resource constraints and to realize their dreams and potential.

* * *

I did not want to limit my work to the education sector forever - there are too many social evils that bother me too much. But I felt I should begin with public education, which is the root, and take up other work as and when we are able to grow our network of volunteers. I had to start somewhere.

So I decided to develop a people-led, volunteer-powered educational campaign. *Edjustice People's Campaign* mobilizes volunteers to contribute 3 to 5 hours a week towards energizing existing government schools and colleges in their own localities, either by organizing development programs or by conducting special sessions and extra-curricular activities. The campaign focuses on activating local social and intellectual resources - doctors, lawyers, current and retired government officials, journalists, sportspersons, and students from reputed institutions - and encourages them to visit impoverished institutions to exchange knowledge in a planned ways. The idea is to supplement what government school and college students get from their teachers, not to interfere with the teaching-learning process in any way but to supplement it. Volunteers take classes on life-skills, offer career counseling, assist awareness about health, and conduct co-scholastic workshops and activities based on sports, arts, culture, and more. Our intention is also to encourage alumni (like myself) to go back and adopt their schools and colleges, and plan their revitalization through informed intervention. After achieving the basic objectives, we seek to strengthen the School Management Committees, with local volunteers helping to organize Parent Teacher Meetings and other programs to improve parent participation, creating a decentralized mechanism for answerability and efficacy in school functioning.

I have designed this model to be replicable and scalable, in any geocultural context.

* * *

The first volunteers we reached out to and organized were from Delhi. But our efforts took flight in my own school, in Katihar. We believed that if we could run a successful pilot in Katihar we could replicate the model across other institutions in Bihar and beyond. Conceptualized around social mobilization and 'individual social responsibility', this model creates a platform, and aims to finally help build student-centric institutions which recognize the uniqueness of each student and gives them opportunities to harness their potential to the fullest. We also envisage eventual support from the government to help institutionalize such efforts, so we can reach out to organizations, individuals, and even corporate social responsibility initiatives more smoothly.

Katihar and my school are just the beginning. A great deal of mobilization needs to be done to rejuvenate stagnating state-run schools and weed out dullness and redundancy in the teaching-learning process. Many friends, colleagues, and volunteers have been kind enough to show their unwavering support and willingness to replicate the model in their hometowns or other preferred locations: this is precisely how the *Edjustice People's Campaign* will turn into a *movement*, an aandolan. And this is an aandolan for young people. For them and to be powered by them. The youth of this country are enthusiastic, fearless, visionaries, all. They have already infused me with such hope - as volunteers and sounding boards through the months and the years. They are this country's greatest resource, and only need to know it.

* * *

As I conclude this particular meditation on my journey so far I am gripped with uncertainty - how much of what I wish to convey through my narrative has in fact been conveyed? If a youth can be distilled into commandments for one's maturer self, and for future work, here are mine.

Education is the key. It is the only tool which can bring about intra-generational change. It holds the answer to the tricky questions of weeding out social evils and facilitating collective progress. Only education aimed and developing human beings into full and diverse versions of themselves has the potential to serve and support their endeavors, as well as to propel us into a more equitable, more balanced, and kinder future. Without simultaneous progress across geographies, communities, genders, and ethnicities the development of the collective human organism is distorted and the entity malformed: we cannot hope to produce harmony in our relations with the earth or with each other without kinship between equals in every local milieu.

Each individual has immense potential and unique talent. It is important to create institutions and norms which enable each citizen to work and progress in accordance with their capacities and interests. Contemporary movements across Europe are facilitating discourse around individuals and the work they do; it is important for us to engage with that discourse, and to adapt it for discussion in and on our society and professional structures. More than anything else, however, it is essential to instill young people with the belief that taking the road less travelled is a fruitful and vital exercise. Each one of them is capable of seeing the big, the bigger, and still bigger picture, and of facing unimaginable challenges (their own or those of others) with faith that there are hundreds of solutions, and combinations of solutions that they can with patience and perseverance set out to follow through on finding solutions to. What they need is one daring talisman: the work they are truly capable of doing, the accomplishments they can stretch themselves to attain to, are important.

Self-progress is not sufficient. We need to take people along. Capable people have the responsibility of strengthening the capacity of others. There is no individual success story: countless unnamed and unknown persons have made everything from table salt to homecooked food possible, which has in turn made late night revisions and the triumph of years-long, physically and mentally strenuous work possible. We can never acknowledge all we owe a debt to. What we can do is hold fast to the precept that wherever we can expand another's potential, we whose beings have been expanded, must.

Respecting women is essential for the progress of any society. No society will be at peace without getting rid of violence and discrimination against women. This has been said in as many million ways as there have been women telling the truth about their oppression - from Leela-ben to the women writers we read in classes on 'women's writing'. It is past time we listened.

Reducing social and economic disparity is a key challenge. This is true for the government as well as for people who are capable of giving back in terms of physical and emotional resources to the society. Assisting those in need is one of our key tasks. Unless we create opportunities for everyone or create a level playing field for those who are far from mainstream development, we cannot think of a just society.

Development of villages and towns is the future. City resources are exhausted and overburdened. We will have to work around creating sustainable and progressive employment opportunities, good quality education and health facilities, safe drinking water, electricity and good connectivity with roads and other effective means of transport. This seeming cliché bears repeating because in all discourse except that centered specifically on 'rural development' it is lost; this essential fact is reduced to a quaintness. It is in fact a terrifically urgent truth that needs immediate attention in our daily lives: we need to support the spaces beyond the cities we live in through everyday choices we make.

Creating immediately accessible ecosystems for change is critical. Standalone efforts can't bring holistic and far-reaching changes in the society. It is important for stakeholders to collectivize efforts and create supportive ecosystems in order to bring about a credible impact. People's groups and the private sector can and should take the lead in such efforts and not just wait for the government to act, lest all positive visions for the future remain wishful thinking.

Ethics in public life are crucial. Our country is suffering due to severe corruption in all sectors. Those who take social responsibility should be capable of discharging it. We need to encourage young students, who are fresh from schools and colleges, to lead programs and debates which intend to reduce corruption, bring about accountability and provoke social action in general public. We also need to refuse, wherever possible, to countenance the little daily corruptions we allow to pass by. Those with the wherewithal to stop an exploitative operative in his tracks can and must prevent the exploitation of those without the resources to do so.

Our time in History is now. Instead of criticizing the past generations, government and society, we should act without losing time. Our place in history will be determined by what happens in our time and through the action we take, or refuse to take. Most important of all, it is only by taking responsibility that we become responsible, and accountable, citizens and human beings. Professionals and friends and family members. The refusal of responsibility is a collective disgrace, and a private tragedy.

* * *

There is a great connect between Katihar and the Kennedy school. While Katihar gave me and would continue to give me practical knowledge and experience, the Kennedy School is now my reference point for theories and models I need to base my ground work on. And human progress necessitates, of course, that we connect theoretical knowledge with practical applications and vice versa.

After spending two decades in direct practice, my current role affords me a 'balcony' moment, where I am looking at the world of implementation through the lens of knowledge. I am able to delve deep and understand the process of knowledge creation better, following interactions with some of the brightest minds on the planet. And all my endeavors coalesce towards the one, urgent preoccupation – contribute back.

Vasudhaiv kutumbakam. The world is your kin.

I have witnessed a sea change in myself on this long road from Katihar to Kennedy and back. At each step, as I kept expanding the concept of bliss beyond my immediate self, I only felt more liberated, lighter, and yet ever more purposeful.

And if this long, impossible road, with unnerving bends and twists, nauseating heights and crippling lows, and unexpected moments of glory and continuing success could be mine, it could be yours too. To each young child of the country, I send hope and a salute – for they say it true when they call you the custodians of the future of mirth, brightness, and grandeur. Do not give up. Dream and dare. Don't forget, education is the key to opening the trickiest locks in the world.

And once you've done enough for yourself, give back. Trust me, there is no greater joy than seeing the fruits of your labor transform someone else's life for the better.

❑❑

better, following interactions with some of the brightest minds on [illegible]